Learning and Discovery

Learning and Discovery

The University and the Development of the Mind

Stephen David Ross
State University of New York
at Binghamton

GORDON AND BREACH SCIENCE PUBLISHERS
New York   London   Paris

Copyright © 1981 by Gordon and Breach, Science Publishers, Inc.

Gordon and Breach, Science Publishers, Inc.
One Park Avenue
New York, NY 10016

Gordon and Breach Science Publishers Ltd.
42 William IV Street
London, WC2N 4DE

Gordon & Breach
7-9 rue Emile Dubois
F-75014 Paris

Library of Congress Cataloging in Publication Data

Ross, Stephen David.
  Learning and discovery.

  Includes bibliographical references and Index.
  1. College teaching. I. Title.
LB2331.R63   378'.125   81-4615
ISBN 0-677-05110-7   AACR2

Contents

Introduction

We are confronted today by a question that has haunted us for most of this century: that of education *for whom* and education *for what*. It is a question fundamentally about teaching and leaning: *who* should learn *what*, and *how* they should be taught. Unfortunately, these questions are frequently obscured by the social and political problems of our time. We read about the organization of the university, its economic difficulties, the expectations and professional goals of the faculty, the vocational and emotional needs of the students, the problems of the world and so on. These are all of great importance but, for a system of education, primarily as they affect *learning*. Yet despite a number of interesting and important writings on cognitive development, language, and the mind over the past twenty years, learning remains as mysterious as ever. I shall argue that in fundamental respects this mystery is intrinsic. However, I do not mean to imply that it is therefore recalcitrant and irrational, but that it requires explicit acknowledgment in our instructional means and educational theories. The paradox of learning found in Plato's *Meno* remains with us today in full force, to be dissipated only after we have understood its seriousness and legitimacy. We cannot learn what we already know, and we cannot learn what we do not understand at all. It is a question of how understanding is to be acquired, how insight is to be attained.

Over the past twenty years, we have seen many writers express extreme hostility to established schools,[1] as well as major transformations in university organization around the world, and a wealth of important theories addressing the powers of the mind.[2] In spite of this, university professors share a justified contempt for education as a subject matter—though they admit by their disdain that none of them has been taught to teach. The problem is that while some university professors may not teach very well, we must assume that students frequently learn a good deal by attending school. The paradox of learning haunts us in the realization that we encounter learning everywhere around us, in our own work as well as our students', yet we have no idea how to teach them to make the discoveries that constitute learning. We can lead them, but we must ultimately rely on their own mental powers.

This essay is not about the university as an institution—political, social, or other. I shall argue that the university ought not to be a single institution, that no one pattern can satisfactorily exemplify the plurality of inventive powers presupposed in higher forms of learning. My argument will emerge from a focus upon the central issue of education—what learning is, and how it may take place. I shall show that it is no accident that teaching is frequently poor and learning sporadic in colleges and universities. It is inherent within the presuppositions and norms of instructional activities. It is grounded in misconceptions concerning the nature of the mind and its cognitive powers. A richer conception of the mind and the nature of understanding can be found in the long philosophical tradition, but also in many recent theories—in particular, Piaget's developmental theory, Chomsky's transformational generative grammar, and in the work of writers in the phenomenological tradition: Merleau-Ponty and Heidegger. I will begin with Plato's *Meno* to establish the basis for the paradox of learning and its possible resolutions, but I will turn to more contemporary theories to define the conditions and principles that are inherent in an adequate theory of the powers of the mind.

Many recent writers have been struck by problems associated with the social and political role of the university, its function as an economic institution.[3] I shall argue that a university that encourages the development of the powers of the mind will be a social and political force needing no other social role, though it will inevitably be given many different roles. Far from encouraging an ivory tower mentality or complicity with economic and social forces, a respect for learning for its own sake must encourage a critical and imaginative stance on all aspects of human life. The view that an educated electorate will make wise and effective political decisions used to be widely held. It seems no longer to bear scrutiny; university graduates are no wiser than other people. My position is that this is largely due to how instruction is carried on in colleges and universities. An educated person ought to be relatively immune to advertising and election campaign lures, less ready to believe the great lies by which a society rationalizes its corruption, more able to develop alternatives and evaluate their consequences. Unfortunately, if one is taught to believe great truths in the same way as one might believe lies, then when it counts, one may not be able to tell them apart.

STEPHEN DAVID ROSS

REFERENCES

1. Ivan Illich: *Deschooling Society,* New York, Harper & Row, 1970; John Holt: *How Children Fail,* New York, Dell, 1964; *How Children Learn,* New York, Dell, 1970; Jonathan Kozol: *Free Schools,* Boston, Houghton Mifflin, 1972.
2. Noam Chomsky: *Cartesian Linguistics,* New York, Harper & Row, 1966; *Language and Mind,* New York, Harcourt, Brace and World, 1968; Jean Piaget: *Genetic Epistemology,* New York, Columbia University Press, 1970; *To Understand is to Invent,* New York, Grossman, 1973; *Psychology and Epistemology,* New York, Viking, 1972.
3. Christopher Jencks *et al.: Inequality: A Reassessment of the Effect of Family and Schooling in America,* New York, Basic Books, 1972; Donald M. Levine and Mary Jo Bane (eds.): *The "Inequality" Controversy,* New York, Basic Books, 1975.

PART I

Learning

CHAPTER 1

The Paradox

Plato's *Meno* begins with the question, "Can virtue be taught?" Inevitably, this question asks us to consider the uniqueness of moral instruction, and Socrates toward the end of the dialogue examines the possibility that virtue may be unlike anything else acquired. Nevertheless, the dialogue also raises the question of whether anything can be taught as well as whether anything can be learned. This is the force of the paradox of learning: that we cannot learn what we already know or understand what we do not know. Learning is impossible here because it presupposes a mixture of knowledge and ignorance which is incompatible with the idea of a clear distinction existing between them.

From this extreme point of view, virtue is not unique in being unteachable. The paradox suggests that nothing can be learned and nothing can be taught. The difficulties involved in moral education often seem insuperable, so that we might be tempted to follow Socrates' lead at the end of the *Meno* and conclude that virtue is neither knowledge nor teachable, but is acquired by divine illumination, except that a similar illumination may be required for all learning.

The claim that nothing can be taught may be based on two quite different principles. First, no one possesses complete and infallible knowledge, so that no one can do more than attempt to communicate what he believes. Socrates asks Anytus toward the end of the *Meno* just who are the teachers of virtue. Who can claim to possess knowledge of virtue and the good life? If we pre-suppose that a teacher is a master, simple scepticism entails that no one may claim himself to be a teacher of virtue.

The second principle is that we are not interested in teaching facts or simple truths alone, but in teaching people to think for themselves, to form their own critical opinions, to judge the claims and arguments of others. A man may memorize and repeat facts told to him, but he does not *know* them until they have become part of his repertoire of argument and under-standing. We wish to teach people to judge and think, to gain methods and skills. But these cannot be taught; they can be learned only by example or through experience. It is a common view that musicians are born, not made, as are mathematicians. But a small part of music and mathematics can be learned by rote. Unless a person has a native gift for mathematics, he cannot be taught it, while if he possesses this gift, he really teaches himself. All a teacher can do is offer examples of thinking and acting, and allow his pupil to go his own way. No one can transmit understanding to someone else and it is then but a short step to the view that reading cannot be taught. Either a child learns to read "on his own," because he is interested, because there are books in his home, because he is "culturally advantaged," or he does not learn to read at all. All instruction is but encouragement, and success is simply the fulfillment of the latent powers of the mind.

A number of recent theories and philosophical discussions are directly relevant to these issues. Relative to the question of fallibility we may note Richard Rorty's strenuous attack on all forms of incorrigibility in knowledge, as not so much mistaken as misconceived.[1] There are no systematic and pervasive grounds for cognitive claims, and neither philosophy nor science can represent or mirror reality. Rorty loosely follows Dewey and Wittgenstein in viewing the classic epistemological tradition as grounded in an illegitimate quest for certainty.[2] While we may agree (conventionally) that certain claims involving pains and sensations are not to be questioned intelligibly, they are not to be considered infallible: all knowledge is fallible, based on the con-ventions and norms of social life. As I will show, an adequate view of learning depends on a theory of fallible and corrigible insights. Any sort of infallibility makes the paradox of learning unresolvable.

The second question, of the ways in which knowledge transcends information and facts, prior experience, goes back to Kant, but can be found expressed more powerfully today in Piaget and Chomsky. In particular, it is essential to their arguments that invention is not only a potentiality inherent in understanding, but a defining criterion of understanding. In Chomsky's words,

The most striking aspect of linguistic competence is what we may call the 'creativity of language', that is, the speaker's ability to produce new sentences, sentences that are immediately understood by other speakers although they bear no physical resemblances to sentences which are 'familiar'. ...Normal use of language involves the production and interpretation of sentences that are similar to sentences that have been heard before only in that they are generated by the rules of the same grammar.[3]

In Piaget's words, which express the conceptual point directly:

...I consider the main problem of genetic epistemology to be the explanation of the construction of novelties in the development of knowledge... for the genetic epistemologist, knowledge results from continuous construction, since in each act of understanding, some degrees of invention is involved; in development, the passage from one stage to the next is always characterized by the formation of new structures which did not exist before, either in the external world or in the subject's mind.[4]

The principle involved here is that *to understand is to invent*. Invention is the criterion that distinguishes mere reproduction and imitation from understanding, which is grounded in principles of organization and rules. Related to the principle of invention is a principle of transcendence: that *learning always transcends the available data, evidence, or instructional materials.* The paradox of learning expresses a profound and fundamental problem of cognitive development when it is understood to address how students are able to go beyond what is presented to them and how they learn to be inventive and creative with their cognitive powers. The point of the principle of invention is that no understanding is possible, however modest and elementary, which does not involve invention, new applications, situations, and insights. The problem of learning is how novel insights can be attained.

A natural—perhaps the most popular—solution is to suppose that novel insights are acquired but not taught, that understanding is therefore acquired but not transmitted. Recent theories of sequential stage development and maturation lend support to this position. Presentation of material before the child is ready tends to be counterproductive. Children who mature later often catch up very rapidly. The Piagetian principle that cognitive development is the outcome of stages, whose sequence is a function of internal conditions, tends to minimize the role of the teacher and the importance of the environment.

What is at stake is the nature of both knowledge and learning. It is plausible to suppose that only imitative activities can be routinely taught and that deeper understanding cannot be transmitted to passive, uncritical, and uninterested students. In addition, no teacher has perfect knowledge: it is therefore plausible to suppose that a teacher can at best inculcate an imperfect understanding in his pupils, essentially by memorization and repetition.

The position that nothing can be taught has important political ramifications. It is obvious that some learning, however trivial it may be, does take place. It is also obvious that some children do not learn what their teachers attempt to teach them in school. The teachers whose students fail may relieve themselves of responsibility by denying that they could have done better. *Nothing can be taught.* All that can be done is to present materials and to encourage the child through patience and discipline. If he does not learn, then he is at fault. It is his own attitudes or native incapacities which make him incapable of learning. A related position is that, since nothing can be taught, the schools should be closed. Teachers are not needed; what is required instead is a flexibly-structured society in which young people are exposed to a variety of experiences to learn what they will from them.[5]

The view that learning occurs essentially without teaching leads to a common disparagement of instructional methods and a disdain for education as a discipline. A person may study a branch of knowledge but not how to teach. Teaching is then either the assertion of known facts or a natural gift which has no rationale or methodic control. A subject can be learned, but how it is presented is essentially irrelevant. The explanation of learning does not lie in the teacher, but in the student, and the former's role becomes largely mysterious and unintelligible.

This discussion has presupposed that although nothing can be taught, human beings can learn. Our reading of books, our heeding of arguments, even our claim that learning is impossible are all grounded in the possibility of learning. Yet the issues of teaching and learning are not separable, since they depend on some of the fundamental properties of the mind and of its powers. The paradox of learning entails that both teaching and learning are impossible, though we are apparently surrounded by learning on all sides. I will approach these matters through a detailed examination of the *Meno* where the central issues are posed in striking form. Not the least part of the presentation is the irony which pervades the dialogue, continually asking us to reexamine the claims made and resolutions proposed.

The *Meno* begins with the question, "Can virtue be taught?" As is his wont, Socrates inverts the question and claims that he cannot answer until he knows what virtue is. He therefore asks Meno to define it. After a few simple failures, Meno becomes quite exasperated. The first time, Socrates reassures him by giving him an example of an adequate definition, and defines *figure* as "that which always follows color". Meno is not satisfied, and demands a further definition. At this point, and seemingly only in passing, Socrates offers an extremely important response to the question of what he would say to someone who claimed he did not know what color is.

I should have told him the truth. And if he were a philosopher of the eristic and antagonistic sort, I should say to him: You have my answer, and if I am wrong, your business is to take up the argument and refute me. But if we were friends, and were talking as you and I are now, I should reply in a milder strain and more in the dialectician's vein; that is to say, I should not only speak the truth, but I should make use of premises which the person interrogated would be willing to admit. And this is the way in which I shall endeavor to approach you.[6]

This passage merits considerable attention. It expresses important features of Socrates' method and reveals a fundamental aspect of his theory of education. But in important and specific ways it is also relevent to the dialogue and its implications.

We must recall Meno's initial question: "Can virtue be taught?" Is this a question that would arise in a normal conversation as an expression of genuine puzzlement? It is difficult to see how. A plausible suggestion is that Meno has heard both the question and various answers from Gorgias, and is posing an examination for Socrates. Socrates considers him presumptuous as well as incompetent, and redirects the proceedings. Instead of being examined, Socrates becomes the examiner.

But a more important transformation takes place in the first part of the dialogue. According to my suggestion, Meno's first question is not a sincere one. He does not ask it in order to learn from the answer but to judge Socrates' abilities and to show off his own. In replying with a question, and claiming that he does not know what virtue is, Socrates establishes a situation of inquiry to replace an examination of credentials. The *Meno* is about education as much as virtue, and the first business at hand within the dialogue is to create the possibility of learning.

Thus, in the passage given just above, Socrates is making an important distinction. If a man engages in discussion in bad faith—that is, not willing to learn, but in an antagonistic and disputatious frame of mind—then the appropriate thing to do is to beat him at his own game. Challenge him; puncture his smugness; force him to reveal his strengths and weaknesses. A smug person cannot be taught anything, for he is too sure of himself to consider questions deeply and to engage in the necessary self-criticism. He must be challenged; his self-assurance must be shaken; he must be shown the limitations of his views. He cannot learn unless he is openminded and receptive. Learning is incompatible with complacency. We have here one explanation of why there can be teaching without learning—when the student is closedminded, unaware of his ignorance and unreceptive to new ideas. We also have an explanation of why Socrates continually asserts his ignorance: to indicate his openminded, inquiring attitude, to show that he rejects all cognitive authorities who would effectively terminate inquiry. Although the discussion with the slave boy later in the *Meno* is almost entirely ironic, there are two passages which express important Socratic principles. After he has led the boy to admit his ignorance, Socrates points out:

Do you see Meno, what advances he has made in his powers of recollection? He did not know at first, and he does not know now, what is the side of a figure of eight feet: but then he thought that he knew, and answered confidently as if he knew, and had no difficulty; now he has a difficulty, and neither knows nor fancies that he knows.

...Do you suppose that he would ever have inquired into or learned what he fancied that he knew, though he was really ignorant of it, until he had fallen into perplexity under the idea that he did not know, and had desired to know? (*Meno* 84)

A necessary step in learning is receptiveness, the development of an open, inquiring mind, a willingness to consider alternatives.

Meno has begun the discussion in bad faith. Socrates' remarks are directed explicitly at his initial attitude: If you are merely being difficult, then show me that my definition is wrong! When Meno objects to Socrates' definition of "figure" on the grounds that he does not know what color is, he may be beginning an infinite series of questions leading to no possible resolution.

But if Meno is not being merely disputatious, we may begin the business of teaching and learning by making "use of premises which the person interrogated would be willing to admit". So Socrates defines color in a fashion familiar to Meno after his studies with Gorgias: "color is an effluence of form, commensurate with sight, and palpable to sense" (Meno, 76c). Meno's doubts are temporarily laid to rest, and he is willing to continue the discussion: "I will stay, Socrates, if you will give me many such answers" (77a).

Unfortunately, he fares no better with his next definition of virtue, and in exasperation bursts out: "O Socrates, I used to be told, before I knew you, that you were always doubting yourself and making others doubt; and now you are casting your spells over me, and I am simply getting bewitched and enchanted, and am at my wits' end" (80b). Like a torpedo fish, Socrates has thoroughly confused and paralyzed Meno. Meno is bewildered and confused about matters he thought he understood. His exasperation is so great that he cannot continue the discussion. Socrates must again find a common starting-place from which the two of them may pursue their inquiry. However, in his frustration, Meno casts about at straws to show that he is no dunce, and also to divert the discussion from a topic which has begun to threaten him severely, and he proposes the paradox of learning which he has obviously heard mentioned: how can a man learn anything, since if he already knows it he cannot learn it, while if he does not know it, he cannot inquire into what he does not know, and therefore cannot learn. In short, no one can learn anything. Or, put another way, perhaps we may *have* knowledge, but it is impossible to *acquire* it.

The comparison of Socrates to a torpedo fish is very important, for it suggests that learning and inquiry are frequently confusing and paralyzing in certain phases. Against the principle that learning is a continuous passage from confusion to clarity, darkness to light, Plato is suggesting that it proceeds by fits and starts, with periods of confusion necessary to major advances in understanding. The line between ignorance and knowledge is constantly being blurred, producing confusion and bewilderment in the midst of understanding, as we encounter familiar objects and ideas from a novel point of view. This is the major insight required for the resolution of the paradox of learning. What is involved is a change in *viewpoint,* not simply the accumulation of additional information. There are important similarities here with the theses of Kuhn and Piaget, wherein later phases of understanding replace earlier ones in a complex, non-linear progression.[7] A change in paradigm, logical system, or general viewpoint is required, and this will frequently produce confusion where the transition from one organizing perspective to another is involved. A change in perspective, paradigm, or general theory offers a natural mixture of confusion and understanding where advances in knowledge produce temporary bewilderment. Meno complains that Socrates paralyzes his mind. Such a paralysis may be a normal condition of all major advances in understanding.

Socrates' explicit reply to the paradox of learning is given in the doctrine of recollection. We cannot acquire knowledge, so we must always have possessed it, and only had it slip from our minds. I will take up the doctrine of recollection in the next sub-chapter. Before doing so, it is important to consider the paradox somewhat further. On the surface, it reaches an absurd con-clusion — that nothing can be learned. Yet it addresses some profound problems of education and the theory of knowledge.

The absurdity of the paradox can be easily demonstrated. It is presented in the form of a dilemma, and may be replied to by a counter-dilemma. If Socrates has no answer to the paradox, then he has learned its truth; if he has an answer, then Meno will learn it. In either case, something will be learned. The absurdity is indicated by Plato in having Meno say, upon Socrates' suggestion of the doctrine of recollection: "Can you teach me how this is?" And if we are not completely convinced of the ridiculousness of the entire discussion, Socrates explains the doctrine of recollec-tion by proposing that "the soul has learned all things", and says of the slave boy later, "if he did not acquire the knowledge in this life, then he must have had and learned it at some other time" (85e). The hypothesis is that the soul had *learned* what it knows in a former life, which is no solution to the paradox of learning. Socrates is pulling Meno's leg; Plato is pulling ours at the same time. Any dialogue, discussion, or tract presupposes that the participants and audience may learn something. Socrates' conclusion, "that we shall be better and braver and less helpless if we think that we ought to inquire than we should have been if we indulged in the idle fancy that there was no knowing and no use in seeking to know what we do not know" (86b), is the only principle to accept if inquiry and reason are to prevail.

Counter-dilemmas are rhetorical devices; they do not explore substantive issues. We must unravel the dilemma horn by horn. The first argument is that a man who has knowledge cannot inquire. This is in some sense true. But consider the beginning of the *Meno* once more. Meno begins the dialogue quite sure of his knowledge of virtue although he does not know what virtue is. He must be puzzled first in order to inquire. Ignorance masquerades as knowledge in order to stifle inquiry. The first step in learning is to accept the possibility of error and to be critical of oneself as well as of others. A man who has knowledge will not and need not inquire. But no one in any of the Platonic dialogues has this knowledge, and the question may be raised as to whether anyone could have a knowledge that would make inquiry unnecessary. Socrates constantly asserts his ignorance, in part to disarm his disputant, but also to show that he is openminded, that he is engaged in inquiry.

Consider further the difference between true opinion—which Socrates asserts with a smile is certainly *true*—and knowledge. In the *Meno,* the difference is characterized in terms of the assurance provided by knowledge. In the *Theaetetus,* knowledge is true opinion plus an *account.* In both cases, it is essential to inquire into one's own opinions not only as to whether they are true, but as to their foundations. Knowledge is distinguished from true opinion by the arguments which support it, the investigations performed and the questions answered. Although it is true in a sense that *if* one has knowledge he need not inquire, we can have such knowledge only by inquiry.

We may note here Heidegger's remark that "to know means to be able to learn", to ask questions in an open way.[8] A man who has knowledge cannot use it to justify ceasing to inquire, but possesses his knowledge only by virtue of continuing to raise questions. We may, therefore, deny the truth of the statement that "a man who possesses knowledge has no need to inquire". Given the Platonic sense of dialogue and the recurrent nature of its dialectic, it is far truer to say that a man can possess knowledge only by inquiry, and ceases to have knowledge as soon as he ceases to question. Knowledge is not a possession or state of being, but is the outcome of an activity. Education here is the process of coming to know through inquiry.

The other horn of the paradox is that a man who is ignorant cannot tell when he has learned what he has been taught, nor if it is true. There is, of course, a way of learning facts that is not affected by this argument — the parroting or rote memorization of truths told to us by another person which we accept on his authority. Most of what is taught in schools is through rote learning without inquiry. The question raised by the paradox is how and when such memorization can be transformed into knowledge. This is Kant's question, and he argues that reproduction and memory can never become knowledge without transcendent principles possessed by the mind itself.

We may again consider the difference between knowledge and true opinion. Opinions, true or not, may be acquired by memorization, by following an authority. It is true today and was true at Plato's time that a major part of what we have learned was taught us in this way. But we have then been taught only opinions, however true they may be. We have come to knowledge only when we possess the "account" mentioned in the *Theaetetus* — proof, explanation, interpretation, analysis, or principles of interconnection: something "beyond" the acquired opinions which imbues them with understanding. Knowledge transcends belief and understanding transcends the materials out of which it is fashioned. The question is what we must postulate as the transcendent conditions of the mind that enable us to move from what we encounter to understanding. At the very least, understanding is reached when we can interpret and analyze what is known in addition to being able to repeat it. The paradox of learning essentially dismisses the bare facts, which are so large a part of schooling, as being of little or no consequence. I too shall dismiss facts as relatively inconsequential in an adequate theory of education, and I shall explain why.

The second horn of the paradox may now be restated, not with respect to memorization by rote, but with respect to knowledge. Can a man be brought to knowledge from ignorance, or does this very ignorance make him incapable of judging the truth of the principles or facts which he must consider as candidates for knowledge? In pedagogical terms, if education begins with facts acquired by rote, how can a student develop the capacity for critical judgment? This is the fundamental problem of education: how human beings can be brought to rational understanding. We have identified two relevant principles: that the line between knowledge and ignorance is essentially blurred, based on a process of inquiry; and that knowledge is transcendent, going beyond the materials presented and based on invention.

It is time to consider Plato's own solution to the problem of learning, the doctrine of recollection with many of its more contemporary forms. In the *Meno,* however, irony triumphs over the theoretical issues, for we are presented with an account of this theory in its most absurd form. We will have to interpret Plato's words as best we can, guided by an account suffused with mockery even of itself.

CHAPTER 2

Recollection

The doctrine Socrates proposes for resolving the paradox of learning is that "as all nature is akin, and the soul has learned all things, there is no difficulty in her eliciting, or as men say 'learning', out of a single recollection, all the rest, if a man is strenuous and does not faint; for all inquiry and all learning is but recollection" (81c). I have noted the irony in this formulation, for we cannot resolve the paradox of learning by presupposing that "the soul has learned all things".

The scene is well known in which Socrates "teaches" Meno's slave the length of the line which is the side of a square double the area of a given square. Commentators have frequently read it with great seriousness. Yet the scene is truly laughable. Socrates asks the boy fifty-three questions — with numerous asides to Meno, as if the slave were not present — of which all but eleven are leading questions to which the boy answers only yes or no. Of the remaining eleven, eight are arithmetical: "How many are twice two feet?" "How much are three times three feet?" The three questions which are neither trivial nor leading are all about the correct line. The boy first answers the question incorrectly, the second time admits that he does not know the answer, and finally, led by the nose to count squares in a diagram drawn by Socrates, finds the correct line. Socrates now turns to Meno and asks, "Were not all these answers given out of his own head?" And while we collapse laughing, Meno solemnly admits, "Yes, they were all his own".

The ironies of this exchange are multiple. First of all, it is ironic that Socrates, who so frequently scorns lawyers and rhetoricians, should engage in a mode of interrogation that a clever lawyer might use to manipulate a witness and which any competent lawyer would object to strenuously. Leading questions are treacherous and are no way to arrive at the truth on any subject. We must suppose both Plato and Socrates knew this quite well.

Second, the slave boy exchange is a formidable satire on the Socratic method which frequently appears manipulative and patronizing. The Socratic method is a powerful means of instruction, but not simply because of its question and answer form, which can be easily distorted and abused. Rather, it can be effective only when it is inquiry, based on fundamental principles of understanding and insight. The method requires active thought and outspoken criticism. It makes the regurgitation of facts entirely unacceptable. Yet it is absurd to suppose that what is sought lies buried in the student's mind, to be brought forth in response to questions.

If the explicit argument in the *Meno* for the doctrine of recollection is indefensible, must we conclude that Plato has no solution to the paradox of learning? Or should the doctrine of recollection be interpreted nevertheless as his fundamental solution? Philosophers from Descartes to Kant, Piaget to Chomsky, have argued that some form of knowledge must be presupposed in the fundamental conditions of the mind if knowledge is to be the result. However, we may recall two of Socrates' remarks in the dialogue: "I should make use of premises which the person interrogated would be willing to admit" and "we shall be better and braver and less helpless if we think that we ought to inquire than we should have been if we indulged in the idle fancy that there was no knowing" (86c). Socrates has found a means for persuading Meno to listen through premises which the latter will accept. All well and good; and perhaps we may conclude that even false premises, absurd arguments, and colorful myths may be useful devices for persuading an obstreperous student. But

Socrates also claims that the premises must be true. What is the truth in the doctrine of recollection?

The problem the doctrine addresses is how learning is possible, how human beings can reach a knowledge which is more than true opinion. Alternatively, the problem is how *understanding* may replace *repetition*. It is how understanding and invention are possible, how one learns to transcend what one is told and to make it one's own.

One of the difficulties facing us is of defining what we are contrasting with mere opinion: "understanding", "insight", "comprehension". Intuition has frequently been described in miraculous, ineffable terms, almost mystically, as a divine illumination which cannot be described much less explained. I have noted the striking convergence of principles in certain recent theories that understanding involves invention and transcendence, but there is considerable difference of opinion on the scope and kind of invention and departure that must be taken into account. It is worth noting here Wittgenstein's denial that there is anything in particular more to understanding than being able to give the right answer. He asks, for example, what it means to know the principle of a series: 1, 2, 4, 7,...? He answers: many things — to be able to give the next number; to be able to state the principle upon which the series is constructed; and so forth.[9] He is attacking the view that there is an inner criterion essential to "knowing" the principle of such a series. In this respect he is certainly correct. There is an equally striking proof of this conclusion in the *Theaetetus*. If an internal assurance is required for knowledge, then either we have it and error is impossible; or if error is possible, then we have no such assurance. But no proof can be guaranteed to be infallible as the frequency of human error shows. Therefore, no inner guarantees are possible, since they would either require further guarantees that one had had the experience which provided assurance, and an infinite number of them, or they would eliminate error.

The issue we are concerned with is what more there is to understanding than being able to give the correct answer. Wittgenstein shows that no specific condition can differentiate knowledge from belief, understanding from repetition. Nevertheless, answers may be given in confusion or by rote. True opinion is not knowledge and should not be encouraged to masquerade as knowledge. Yet no specific internal criteria of psychic certainty can be found to distinguish true opinion from knowledge. Opinions come with all the appropriate insignia of knowledge, except that they are not known. We look to arguments, proofs, and evidence to distinguish opinions from knowledge, though these do not provide absolute guarantees either. However, even a proof requires something more than the steps of the argument which can be memorized. It also requires "seeing" or "understanding" that the steps constitute a proof. Separate items must be "seen" to form a whole. Either we can "see" or we cannot know; and if we do not "see", how are we to be made to understand? The paradox of learning is with us again. Either we sense the structure of numbers and proofs or we do not. Without such a sense, no further argument is possible. If we possess such a sense, we are not taught to have it.

We may return to the doctrine of recollection. It addresses the problem of learning as just defined — the learning which depends on insight. The paradox of learning may be restated as follows: either a person possesses insight or he does not. In no case can he be taught it or learn it, though he may acquire it. While this version of the paradox may have no solution, we must still suppose that learning is possible. We must therefore make plausible some sense of *vision* or *insight*. This is the purpose of the doctrine of recollection. All versions of innate ideas, including Chomsky's universal grammar, rest on the assumption that cognitive invention and transcendence cannot be derived from repetition alone, so we must presuppose cognitive structures and principles out of which new principles may emerge. We effectively presuppose a version of Kant's principle: *facts without insight are unintelligible; insight without facts is absurd.*

The doctrine of recollection is grounded on an important analogy: the capacity of the mind to "see" truth, to gain insight, is like that of the mind to remember. In both cases, no proof can be given — of insight or memory. Any proof would presuppose what it sought to prove — that we could understand the proof or that we could remember evidence or argumentative steps in sequence. The doctrine of recollection assimilates insight to memory in the form of an analogy. Neither is provable. Both must be taken for granted as necessary features of learning and knowing. Both are central to the theory of knowledge, which can challenge them only at its peril. Both are essential features of all knowledge.

Neither memory nor insight is a mystery in the sense of being unanalyzable, though they must be presupposed to exist and to be veridical prior to their analysis. Psychology makes vital contributions to the theory of education in its study of the general traits of both memory and insight. Unfortunately, the contemporary university has in many ways found it necessary to replace insight by memory. The analogy between intuition and memory can be perverted. In later chapters, I shall explore this perversion in detail. But I must first lay the groundwork for my analysis. It is essential that we avoid a conception of insight which is mysterious and obscure, for there are insights to be encountered everywhere in experience.

CHAPTER 3

Insight

A later chapter will be devoted to a detailed analysis of insight and discovery in relation to learning. Here I will simply examine several paradigms of insight, for we need no technical theory to reveal the impoverishment of much university education. The well-founded expectation that insights will come in time can be transformed into the perverse assumption that insight is irrelevant to educational practices. It may even be discouraged in the classroom. Yet every student must attain insights on his own.

A traditional paradigm of insight is that of geometry. It is a useful one not only because of its rigor and precision, nor even based on a sense of mathematical order in the universe, but because many of the most fundamental types of insight are embodied clearly there. I suggest that all the important types of insight have some function in geometry. The lesson to be learned from this is not that geometry is unique, but that fields of learning are based on complex modes of understanding. In the following discussion I will not endeavor to exhaust the modes of insight, nor to analyze the requirements of various branches of knowledge. I will merely describe a single study to exhibit its visionary aspects.

The two most striking features of geometry are the step-by-step character of deductive proof and the comprehensive structure of space. Consider first the nature of a proof. We begin with a set of axioms, a number of propositions in either a natural or formal language. Several other propositions are written down which "follow from" the axioms. Finally, we conclude with a proposition which represents the theorem we set out to prove. To all outward appearances, a deductive proof is merely a sequence of statements concluding with the theorem "proved". Embodied in such a scheme, however, are a number of different modes of insight.

Steps

Descartes' *Fifth Rule for the Guidance of our Native Powers* is as follows:

Method consists entirely in the orderly handling of the things upon which the mind's attention has to be concentrated, if any truth bearing on them is to be discovered. We shall comply with it exactly, if we resolve involved and obscure data step by step into those which are simpler, and then starting from the intuition of those which are simplest, endeavour to ascend to the knowledge of all the others, doing so by corresponding steps (taken in reverse order).[10]

From a sceptical vantagepoint it is appropriate to ask if there are indeed "simple" steps which can be intuited. But from our point of view, in which we take knowledge and deductive proof for granted, Descartes' description is apt. There must exist steps in deductive proofs which can be intuited, which are in that sense "obvious". Mathematicians and logicians routinely tell their classes that such and such a theorem is "obvious". This infamous obviousness reveals two features of the insight belonging to step-by-step activity: some steps must be apprehended to follow from others if any step-by-step method is possible; what is obvious differs from person to person. At an extreme, some insights are false. Yet the fallibility of insight does not inhibit its powers and necessity. Insight is necessary to a criterion of understanding but not to a criterion of truth. Paradoxically, then, understanding is compatible with error. This is an essential premise needed for the resolution of the paradox of learning.

The analysis of complex steps into simpler ones and the building up of complex steps out of simpler ones are essential cognitive activities. In both cases, rote learning is of limited value, since we must continuously apply the techniques acquired by rote in new contexts and in new ways. The very notion of a "technique" carries the weight of novelty and transcendence within it, since a technique is employable in many ways beyond the contexts in which it was acquired.

We may consider, here, some relatively straightforward ways of acquiring complex insights from simpler steps and their relations. One is essentially habitual, where we have performed sequences of steps so often that we form a habit of inference or formulate a guiding principle which replaces a long sequence of simpler steps by a smaller number of complex steps. It may appear that such a rule of inference can be acquired by rote, without understanding its relational functions. This is an error: habits and guiding rules must be applied in new ways and to new subject matters which transcend their rote conditions. Even here, then, insight into situations and the applications of habits and rules is essential. Nevertheless, as a principle becomes habitual, we come to "see" its application directly.

Not only does geometry require such step-by-step insights, from simpler to complex and conversely, but it may employ a very different mode of insight to achieve the same ends: into the complex geometrical relations which step-by-step activities are directed to display. In both cases, we are led to understand the truth of the theorems involved in complex inferences, but in one case a truth is apprehended as "provable by other inferential steps", and in the other as "true of lines and points" by virtue of the structural character of the geometrical system.

What is involved here is a difference between a "mathematical" and a "logical" intuition—between insight into the relational characteristics of the domain described by the axioms of the system, and insight into the inferential relations among complex propositions of the domain. The same kind of distinction can be realized in a partly-formalized discipline such as physics. A theoretical physicist must formalize his claims in a complex mathematical system. Nevertheless, we may distinguish the insights such a physicist may have into the physical laws that follow mathematically or inferentially from the fundamental postulates of relativity theory from an intuition into the structure of the physical world. The different insights provide different kinds of understanding, though the systems arrived at explicitly may be the same in both cases.

The insights I have described as essential to inferential steps are necessary to all methodic activities, not merely to deductive proof. A painter who paints a canvas sequentially, or an author who begins his novel on page one and then goes on to page two, both require insight into the relations between successive sequential steps, though such steps are not related logically. Each allows earlier steps to impose constraints upon later activities: of consistency, contrast, internal tension, and compatibility. In all such cases, the individual steps may be made intelligible by a sense of the totality realized in the successive steps. A sense of overarching structure may govern subsidiary insights into step-by-step methodic activities.

Wholes

The insight that a given step of a proof is valid has two elements: that the step is valid, and that it is a consistent element of the proof *as a whole*. We have considered the first. The second is probably more what people who speak of intuition have in mind — for example, Bergson's intuition of the individual whole as distinct from its analytic elements.[11] However, there is no reason why intuition should be assigned a purely synthetic role, since analysis also involves insight.

For our purposes, Bergson makes an important point — that analysis always involves synthetic insights. Analytic steps are taken either in the context of a sense of the whole of which they are elements or according to a general rule or method. A random sequence of valid deductive steps does not constitute a *proof* — not, at least, of a particular theorem. A sense of the whole is inherent in a proof as a proof. The replacement of insight by routine methods of computation in no way eliminates the importance of the vitality of the insight required for the proof of a given theorem. Computations according to rule can provide at best an infinite number of theorems among which we must choose those of worth or importance. We again require insight into the entire system of theorems to discern which of its components have value. An element is an element of a totality; and only by a sense of the whole can we grasp the character of one of its elements. Insight is necessary to all sophisticated systems such as those in science and mathematics.

In its most powerful forms, the holistic sense is one of *structure,* an insight into a whole which possesses forms and principles. In an equally general sense, it is insight into the relationship of *belonging,* a grasp of what an element *belongs to.* Without this insight, the human mind would be incapable of inference or of methodic activity. Deductive inferences are given in steps, and require a sense of the proof as a whole for the meaning of each step. Inductive inferences require a sense of the whole process in time through which particular steps are taken, through which experiments are performed, through which we live in expectation.

The two fundamental modes of insight which have been discussed may be given a single description as the elements and structures involved in the relationship of belonging. I will now briefly characterize several other forms of insight which enter into the understanding of complex relations, still using geometry as a major paradigm.

Recognition

In order that any insight be possible, we must be able to recognize the elements involved. We may discriminate three important modes of recognition: (a) *symbols* — essential to mathematics, but also to all codes, language systems, and indirect cognitions, clearly essential to all complex modes of understanding; (b) *perception* — the recognition of something as it appears; (c) *memory* — a fundamental and paradigmatic mode of insight. Not only do we remember events of the past and facts we have learned; not only must we presuppose remembrance of the past in all that we do or know; but all proofs and methods consist of steps, and past steps are presupposed in later ones. Memory is shown to be a form of insight in that it can be trained yet is always immediate.

Anticipation

In all activities through time there is the possibility of intentional direction which depends on insight into the relationship of means to ends. In taking a step, we anticipate the further steps that may follow. In proposing an aim to be realized through activity, we anticipate the steps we may take to reach our aims. In the consideration of an event, we anticipate the consequences that may follow through time. Closely related are insights into *method* — the sequential structure of directed activity; *transcendence* — the possibilities, implications, and connections relevant to any sphere of understanding; *kinship* — similarities and differences; rightness; appreciation; novelty. All of these forms of insight are required in all rich forms of understanding, and understanding presupposes that the relevant modes of insight are available.

The central properties of insight are immediacy, relationality, and fallibility. Insights can be trained and developed, but such development both presupposes other insights and attains a non-mediated form of apprehension. Insight is relational, involving connections and possibilities. But it can also be in error, and must continually be checked — of course, relative to and by means of other insights.

The question, then, for education is how complex, sophisticated, novel, and transcendent insights can be acquired and transmitted, inculcated and developed. Many answers have been proposed to this question, ranging from detailed programs to theories of coding systems and organizing schemas. At one level, the question requires an empirical, psychological answer, which I believe is not known to us today in general. On another level — the one I shall pursue — the question calls our attention to the pervasiveness of invention, novelty, transcendence, and personality in all forms of insight and understanding. The question here is whether our instructional systems and fields of knowledge adequately reflect the role of insight in the acquisition of knowledge. I will trace the implications of this question for the modern university and for the fields of knowledge which inhabit it.

The conclusion to be drawn from the examples given above (it will be discussed in greater detail in Part III) is that understanding requires insight. It follows that learning cannot be regarded as the simple acquisition of facts: cognitive acquisition is never simple; facts themselves are constituted in part by insights (see Chapter 5). Learning is therefore always a form of discovery in which acquired insights involve a transformation of understanding under the control of novel insights. Only through discovery — by following the pathway of interrogation and inquiry — can knowledge be acquired and assimilated to the agent. We can memorize what we are told and repeat it when asked (though even this requires insight into conditions and appropriate responses) but we *understand* what we remember only when we also understand its connections and relations, when it is part of a system of insights and applications. Learning is discovery because it requires adjustment over an indefinite range of insights. One of the implications of this proposition is that learning is in principle fundamentally the same for student and for expert, differing only in the kind of discoveries sought and in acquired capacities to understand. Insight, invention, and understanding are required in all learning, in all discoveries. Too sharp a distinction between student learning and advanced discoveries distorts our understanding of cognitive development and makes it unintelligible. Similarly, too elitist an emphasis on extraordinary students with brilliant minds neglects the pervasiveness of insight, the inventions and understanding attained by everyone who studies and learns.

I am arguing not that learning *ought* to be discovery, but that it *is*, and that we implicitly assume such insight and discovery throughout all phases of instruction, but especially at the university level. However, though understanding requires insight, the relevance of insight has not been explicitly accepted in all university activities. When it has been considered explicitly, as in the English honors system, it has been the mainstay of elitism and stratification rather than a principle essential to learning and instruction of every kind and at every level. The paradox of learning haunts many of the activities and conceptions of university faculty and administrators. The modern university effectively says one thing and believes another. This has created fundamental difficulties for contemporary higher learning, manifested in tensions that turn on economy, scale, and egalitarianism.

CHAPTER 4

The Problem of Insight

In Hermann Hesse's deeply philosophical novel *Das Glasper-lenspiel (The Glass Bead Game)*, Joseph Knecht is "called" to Castalia—as he is called to every further stage of his life and education—to increasing responsibilities, even to his legendary death. By this word, Hesse marks a distinction between an education available to everyone, so uniform and inconsequential as to merit no comment, and the lure of a spiritual life for those who awaken to its magic. Hesse's description of the consequences of Knecht's awakening is:

that hour nevertheless clearly separated the past from the present and the future—just as an awakened dreamer, even if he wakes up in the same surroundings that he had seen in his dream, cannot really doubt that he is now awake. There are many types and kinds of vocation, but the core of the experience is always the same: the soul is awakened by it, transformed or exalted, so that instead of dreams and presentiments from within a summons comes from without.[12]

Such a description is remarkable. But Joseph Knecht is an exceptional person. He becomes not only Master of the Game, but a memorable leader and teacher around whom an important legend develops. Nevertheless, allowing for the literary qualities of the description and the exceptional character of Knecht, Hesse's account of the call to a spiritual ideal is a penetrating portrayal of the qualities of a major insight. A novel insight into

28

something only vaguely imagined before is indeed an awakening, and one is never the same again. One's surroundings are enhanced and suffused with qualities awakened by the vision. A geometrical insight brings one to a new sensitivity to structure, order, proof, and rationality. An artistic vision colors one's entire perception of the world, every sensory encounter, even while the content of the vision remains inchoate and vague.

The paradox of learning confronts us again in a new form. Either the vision essential to learning is available only to a special few, or a capacity for vision is inherent in all minds. If the first alternative is true, teaching may virtually be neglected. In effect, those who can learn will do so; those who cannot will not. School is merely a convenient place for distinguishing among individuals of different abilities, not a place which develops insight. Students learn, but they are not taught. Insight and invention are encouraged in the gifted few, disparaged in the rest. Here insight is a component of excellence but is unavailable to the great majority of students, who learn to parrot and repeat, not to understand. The majority of students succeed at best in memorizing some facts and acquiring some skills, enduring the ordeal of schooling until they can leave. Typically, the habitual dispositions inculcated in these students are hindrances to greater insights. They acquire skills leading to success in school which are often very different from competence within a domain of understanding or insight into a sphere of knowledge.[13]

The second alternative mentioned is presupposed by all systems of universal compulsory education. It is also presupposed by all democratic political theories. Everyone possesses the capacity to learn. A democratic political system can be successful only if its citizens are intelligent and knowledgeable. Equality of opportunity, even more important to democracy than majority rule, is commonly interpreted to mean equality of education, grounded in an established correlation between economic and educational success.[14]

However, the facts do not seem to support the presupposition. If literacy is defined in terms of practical ability to interpret voting alternatives, to understand political controversies, to evaluate statistical studies relevant to critical political issues, the

United States, along with other major industrial nations, has a sizable illiteracy rate. Education is the largest service industry in the United States, yet large groups of people—the poor, blacks, Spanish-Americans, Indians—regularly fail to succeed in school. Educational failure has become an institutionalized way of life, as schools serve a custodial function for students who must attend them but who are abandoned as unteachable. Compensatory programmes for the poor and disadvantaged do not exhibit any reliable indications of success. While economic success in our society largely depends on educational performance, we are faced with a glut of over-educated, academically trained adults who cannot find work in their chosen profession.

There are sharply conflicting tendencies. On the one hand, ambitious young people are expected to attend a college or university. The university then incurs the obligation to provide them with an appropriate education, largely as if they are consumers who must be satisfied with what they receive. The 1960's saw strong pressures to eliminate specific requirements and to abolish failing grades. On the other hand, as competition increases for scarcer, high-paying jobs, stricter measures of competitive success have emerged and more rigorous requirements and grading systems have been reintroduced. A natural conclusion is that the capacity for insight is the factor distinguishing superior from ordinary students, as if routine memorization might suffice for the latter.

A major factor in this confusion is the acquiescence of the university in the paradox of learning. It is entirely unclear whether colleges and universities can provide effective instructional programs for marginal students, whether there are known procedures for instructing students in the different disciplines and professions in higher education, or whether students do not ultimately acquire whatever knowledge and skills they come to possess largely by themselves, drawing upon classroom and library materials but based finally on their own native capacities. On the one hand, it is claimed that colleges should be more selective, for only the most capable students will understand the complexities and subtleties of the greater fields of knowledge; on the other hand, such elitism closes off the most effective means of social and economic mobility in our society. The paradox of learning underlies the most general difficulty facing institutions of higher learning: no one knows *what* he is supposed to teach and *how,* though both teaching and learning appear to play a central social and economic role in modern society.

The university's implicit acquiescence in the paradoxical aspects of learning can be kept hidden only so long as two conditions obtain:

1) *only a small proportion of young people are expected to attend the university.* Here higher education is for very few — either the rich who can afford it, the brilliant who are called to it by some miraculous process, or those few who seek an over-protected life of study. It is by no means necessary that the university be thought of generally as a desirable place to be — in fact, a general sense of suspicion may protect the university, as convents and monasteries are protected by their isolation.

2) *the function of the university within society at large must be clearly if arbitrarily well-defined.* It must be a place for the professional education of doctors and engineers, a watering-place for the sons and daughters of the rich before they take on their family and business responsibilities, or a testing-ground for the elite who will enter public service. It is even possible that the university may have *no* function, provided this is generally accepted.

When the first condition is no longer satisfied, the university inevitably becomes a clearing ground for vocational success, and is expected to serve the varying needs of many and different kinds of students. The paradox of learning then becomes unresolvable. Either everyone possesses the innate capacity for a university education — in which case the university should not exclude any-one — or the capacities necessary to a university education are rare, and the university should be closed to those who do not possess them. The paradox becomes evident for students who fail. The more a university education is required for everyone, the more difficult does the issue of failure become. It exhibits our inability to develop powers of the mind which are not native to it.

The second condition supports the first. The more confusion

there is over the function of a university education, and the wider the range of expectations, the more diverse become the kinds of insight necessary to university education. Here the American university has had its unique problems, which have been felt in recent decades throughout the world. If insight is essential to education, and we postulate a wide range and diversity of insights, then when the university attempts to define a particular kind of education appropriate to all its students, it will impose on many of them expectations they cannot (and perhaps should not) meet, though they possess other important capabilities. The process of selection becomes more obviously arbitrary as the function of the university becomes more confused.

In America today, neither condition is satisfied. No one can say what the specific purpose of a university education is or ought to be, and few try. Often the last ones to make the attempt are university professors, who are both too busily engaged in the activities they consider essential to university life and unclear about the worth of their activities to others. Nevertheless, the absence of a clearly defined purpose to university education may be because no such purpose exists. The university has become all things to all men. Even more important, there is no unity to the many fields of knowledge, indicated by the plurality of disciplines and their central methods and insights. There is no science of sciences, no discipline of disciplines, no known systems of rules, criteria, methods, and insights interrelating all the different fields of knowledge.

It is an implicit acquiescence in the paradox of learning that leads so many teachers to acknowledge, as if it were a great virtue, their ignorance of the purpose of the university as a whole. Nothing can really be taught, least of all the unity of all knowledge. The university is therefore a place in which many individuals go about their separate businesses. In a crisis, either they are collectively of good will and find some consensus, or they discover that the university is a cover for the most diverse and disconnected activities and attitudes, lending itself to no rational agreement. The university is constrained on the one hand by the paradox inherent in its own capacity as an institution of learning, and on the other by the extreme expectations in today's world generated in the exercise of this capacity.

The paradox of learning continues to confine our thinking about education. In the rest of this chapter, I will briefly address a few prominent confusions coloring our view of the modern university and show how they emanate from the central paradox of all education: that only some learn, and they do so without being taught.

1) A striking feature of American universities is the unmixed contempt with which most faculty members view the theory of education. There are even those who consider the ability to teach irrelevant to university education. It is sufficient merely to present material, however one does so: it is up to the students to master it. Here we find a complete if tacit acceptance of the principle that nothing can be taught. It can only be presented, as in a book. It is the student's responsibility—based on abilities and motivation—to master the material doled out.

The majority of university professors are probably not so blind to differences in teaching ability among their confreres. But although they recognize superior ability in teaching, they deny that this ability can be taught, even that it can be learned. It is more a native gift, a feature of personality or attitude of mind. Attempts to evaluate the qualities of excellent teaching are often attacked violently—and one could understand why if it were always the poorer teachers who were threatened. But the principle that good teaching is so intangible a virtue as to be unmeasurable seems widespread, and passes easily into the principle that a teacher can do no more than his best. He is not responsible for the failure of his students to learn. This is tantamount to the claim that there exists no method of teaching which can be acquired or employed.

A central confusion runs through the more moderate position I have just described—the confusion inherent in the paradox of learning. It is tacitly acknowledged that there is superior teaching. But it is denied that the principles, criteria, and methods of good teaching can be formulated, even that good teaching can be measured. It follows that we judge good teaching in terms of the performance the teacher puts on, not in terms of the results of his activities. We ignore his success or failure, and concern ourselves with his manner of presentation, his rhetorical flourishes, his public appearances. We judge his skill at teaching by a visit to his classroom, judging him by what he displays rather than by what transpires in the minds of his students. We replace knowledge with rhetoric, in the exact fashion Plato proscribes. And in so doing, we tacitly deny the principle that good teaching is to be defined in terms of what students learn. The teacher teaches; the student learns—but the two activities are disconnected. We are dubious about whether anything can be taught, whether the insights necessary to significant learning can be engendered from without.

2) The central problem for the contemporary university—that a large proportion of young people both desire and expect some form of higher education—has promoted two ways of relieving the pressure. One is curricular diversification, abandonment of any central body of knowledge which every student must master. Specialization makes it impossible to defend the principle that all students ought to know the same subjects. They cannot be expected to learn what their teachers do not know and cannot teach. Students are therefore given a remarkable freedom to pursue their own interests and capabilities. They cannot be expected to acquire insights foreign to their temperaments or prior training. They cannot be taught what they do not come to naturally.

The second way is the separation of educational facilities into university and vocational institutions, academic and professional programs. Leaving aside the inevitable denigration of vocational programs, we may note the explicit acknowledgment that students differ in their abilities and dispositions. Those whose abilities are not conducive to a university education may be taught to become technicians, mechanics, plumbers, or carpenters.

A crucial premise here is that technical skills are routine, far easier to acquire than the inventive powers required in university disciplines. Yet there are no cognitive powers of the mind that do not involve invention, departures from what has been learned, applications to new situations and problems. The question remains of how novel insights are to be attained, how inventive powers are to be engendered in minds that have not yet acquired them.

3) I have noted the central trait of all modern universities, their division into distinct branches of specialization. I consider such sequestration of fields of knowledge both unwarranted and pernicious, though not to be resolved by overkill: the unification of all branches of knowledge under a single system. However, that is not my concern at the moment. What is more important is the conception of knowledge as comprised of discrete and separable insights, distinct and unrelated methods. For if insights are separate, not intrinsically conjoined, both teaching and learning are impossible. It is by the expansion of understanding from familiarity through confusion that learning is accomplished. Examples and facts all are irrelevant if the particular insights they embody are not transferable. The limitations of the transfer of knowledge from one sphere to another are well documented by research, yet invention and insight always depend on such transfers. The organization of a contemporary university into discrete and unconnected disciplines is a repudiation of the principles upon which all learning and discovery rest.

4) Not very long ago, students demanded *relevance* in their studies. This demand has become muted over the past decade, largely due to increased competitive and vocational pressures. In part, the demand was based on a rejection of the political isolation of the university. In further part, however, it was a repudiation of courses which did not directly address students' lives. In effect, the demand for relevance is a repudiation of all strange, esoteric, or abstract insights. Embodied within the demand for relevance is an apparent refusal to be taught what one does not already know of and care about.

We may, however, invert the relationship and interpret the call for relevance as a yearning for insight. Students who desire relevance cannot see the value nor understand the ramifications of their abstract studies. The dispute over relevance is a confrontation with the paradox of learning in a new form. Those who deny that relevance is a significant issue implicitly deny the possibility of communicating the value and significance of

important insights to others. Those who demand relevance substitute content for insight, tacitly acknowledging the impossibility
of gaining a wholly novel understanding.

5) We find the university attacked on all sides because it has
failed to provide wisdom, knowledge of how to live, or vocational
skills for those who need them. In every case, it is not facts which
are missing. No one denies the ability of teachers to teach and
students to learn facts. It is insights which are lost. The desperate
possibility is that teaching is impossible. Insights may neither be
transmitted nor encouraged, especially by teachers of limited
vision. In primary and secondary schools, even many colleges,
teachers who lack insight themselves teach routine activities and
memorized facts. Those who have insight engage it; those who do
not teach others. How in the world can they?

Where a teacher has no insight into reading or arithmetic to
offer, he at least can keep the children busy in his class doing little
tasks. Some children form their own insights in these activities.
Such a method is therefore not a total failure. But what of the
others? Are they brought closer in their mindless tasks to some
comprehension of what they do? It is a natural consequence of
our educational system, and its confusion in the face of the
paradoxical character of learning, that a call to the abolition of
compulsory education should have been sounded. [15]

Meanwhile, the students who have survived mindlessness and
routine come to a university to complete their education. But by
now they have lost the capacity to recognize the insights which
may be offered to them there. Moreover, they are enrolled in
classes of several hundred students, in which scattered insights are
lost like individual grains of sand on the beach. In the few classes
which engage the student's full span of understanding, and
demand the development of major insights, the ordinary student
finds the strain beyond his ability to endure. The confusion and
anxiety inherent in the transformation of insight are new, and the
student shies away from them. Meanwhile, there can be found
the few students born to a university education, for whom it is all
quite natural. The fact that our most creative students survive
every educational system, acquire and produce novel insights,

saves us from the worst consequences of our neglect of understanding and our acquiescence in the paradox of learning.

Meno, when most confused by Socrates' questions, compares him to a torpedo fish who paralyzes his victims. A fundamental challenge to one's vision of the world is paralyzing; yet one will learn from it only by pushing on. Schooling for most people is either the routine acquisition of facts, without the paralysis of a challenged vision, or the easy acquisition of untrammeled insights. Such students are ill-equipped to confront the possibility of a transcendence in vision which all significant learning requires. Once more the paradox of learning raises its head: no preparation leads directly to a major insight. The problem is how we are to come to terms with the transcendent discoveries which are part of all major achievements in learning, and to do so for all in whom we hope to foster understanding.

REFERENCES

1. Richard Rorty: *Philosophy and the Mirror of Nature,* Princeton, Princeton University Press, 1979, especially. Part II.
2. John Dewey: *The Quest for Certainty,* New York, Minton, Balch, 1929; Ludwig Wittgenstein: *Philosophical Investigations,* Oxford, Blackwell, 1963.
3. Noam Chomsky: *Topics in the Theory of Generative Grammar,* The Hague, Mouton, 1966, p. 11.
4. Jean Piaget: *Genetic Epistemology,* p. 77.
5. See Reference 1 of Introduction.
6. *Meno,* 75d.
7. T.S. Kuhn: *The Structure of Scientific Revolutions,* Chicago, University of Chicago, 1962; Jean Piaget: *op. cit.*
8. Martin Heidegger: *An Introduction to Metaphysics,* Garden City, Doubleday, 1961, p. 18.
9. Ludwig Wittgenstein: *The Blue and Brown Books,* Oxford, Blackwell, 1958.
10. Descartes, René: *Rules for the Guidance of our Native Powers,* tr. by Norman Kemp Smith, New York, Modern Library, 1958, p. 21.
11. Henri Bergson: *Introduction to Metaphysics,* Indianapolis, Bobbs-Merrill, 1949.

12. Hermann Hesse: *The Glass Bead Game,* tr. by Richard and Clara Winston, New York, Holt, Rinehart, & Winston, 1969, p. 58.
13. See Holt, *How Children Fail;* Illich, *Deschooling Society.*
14. See Jencks *et al., Inequality.*
15. See Holt, Illich, *op. cit.*

PART II

Knowledge

CHAPTER 5

Facts

The resolution of the paradox of learning lies on the one hand in acknowledgment of the inventive powers of the human mind—grounded here in a theory of insight—and on the other hand in the repudiation of a conception of knowledge as a state or possession carrying its own certification. The paradox is unresolvable when the line between ignorance and knowledge is made hard and fast, for there is then no way to cross it. The resolution lies in treating the line as fundamentally and systematically blurred, so that we are always partly ignorant, partly knowledgeable, engaged in an unending process of thought in which novel questions are continually being asked and new answers proposed.

A rejection of the view that knowledge rests on secure methods or foundations determinable in advance has become widespread recently in many philosophical circles,[1] though it has not penetrated deeply into conventional views of the sciences. One reason for this lack of influence is that there is a sceptical tone to the repudiation of grounds which is inappropriate to the major sciences. The principle of insight formulated in the last chapter—facts without insight are unintelligible; insight without facts is meaningless—is closely akin to one of the major strains that support the rejection of secure grounds of science lying outside human practices and traditions, without the sceptical implications. Kant's view that the rational conditions of conception

41

define secure grounds of cognition passes over into T.S. Kuhn's view that "normal" science depends on an accepted paradigm or conceptual system in which research is carried on and theories are tested and modified.[2] Change of paradigm is "revolutionary", abnormal, precisely because there are no independent criteria for adjudicating between competing paradigms, Richard Rorty, largely following Wittgenstein, has argued that the search for epistemological foundations is misconceived, based on a naive picture theory of the relationship between language and the world, and that the complex ways in which facts and theories are constituted by language, which is itself constituted by human practices and social life, require us to abandon independent criteria for cognitive claims.[3] Derrida and Heidegger, based on the pervasiveness and constitutiveness of language in what we say about things, argue that language can be responded to only by more language, and that cognitive criteria independent of language and human traditions are unintelligible.[4]

Most of these views emphasize language as a condition of knowledge. Many of them appear profoundly sceptical since there are no grounds outside of language and theory for adjudicating among conflicting theoretical claims. The emphasis on language seems to me misplaced since largely the same position follows from the paradox of learning which requires us to blur the line between ignorance and knowledge if cognitive development is to be intelligible. But such a step must be taken from both sides. Not only must we abandon the notion of complete ignorance, emphasizing the native organizing and cognizing powers of the mind, but we must also abandon the notion of a knowledge grounded on entirely adequate conditions. Ignorance and knowledge are always admixed, ranging from native cognitive powers of perception in the young child to the incompleteness of all knowledge and understanding at the frontiers of science. If there are conditions establishing claims as justified, true, and therefore known, we must *understand* the conditions, and that they have been met, in order to undestand the claims they justify. Wittgenstein's and Derrida's arguments may then be interpreted to show that understanding the conditions that establish validity is unending and interminable: that knowledge is always enmired in a continuing project of reconstitution and reinterpretation.[5]

From this point of view, the suggestion by some contemporary scientists that we will soon exhaust the nature of the physical world is absurd. We will certainly never know all the facts about the physical universe, for there are far too many. The suggestion must therefore refer not to the plurality of specific facts, but to the basic and fundamental laws of the universe. The claim is therefore selective and normative: we will soon know everything *important* about the physical universe. Such a claim neglects entirely the constitutive role played by the mind, overlooking the inexhaustible range of developments in the reconstitution of physical theories based on logical, mathematical, linguistic, cognitive, and philosophical considerations. Not only are such cognitive transformations inexhaustible—an inexhaustible range of variations in conception and interpretation—but so also is the social, even the natural, environment which includes them. The fundamental laws of nature must effectively include within their purview the powers of the human mind and the insights and discoveries it attains. It is absurd that all the fundamental laws of physics might be known, since they would have to encompass the physical laws governing psychic and cognitive activities also, and such applications and extensions are infinite and inexhaustible. But I do not need to defend this stronger thesis here: the grounding of cognitive claims in the investigatory practices of individuals and social groups is the fundamental point that is shared by the writers mentioned above and by any attempt to resolve the paradox of learning, including the theory of insight.

The resolution of the paradox of learning lies in a theory of insight—which I consider the truth inherent in the doctrine of recollection—and in the continual activity of inquiry. Cognitive claims are established by and grounded in the inquiries that surround them. If we generalize this notion to include art and philosophy as well as the rest of the humanities under a notion that does not commit us to proofs, evidence, theory, and data, we are led to a notion of *query* of which inquiry is a species.

Query is the genus of which inquiry is a species... We shall think of query as a process expectative of or inclusive of invention. And we shall think of invention as the methodical process of actually producing in consummation of query.[6]

Query includes the methodic and interrogative activities of artists as well as agents, politicians as well as athletes. It therefore includes all the cognitive powers of the mind. Query is inventive, interrogative, and methodic; it is also ongoing and interminable. The resolution of the paradox of learning lies in the activities of query upon which knowledge is grounded. Cognitive claims are both established by query and validated by query. They are also interpreted by query and augmented by further query. Learning is produced by the activities of query, and only such activities can produce the discoveries that culminate in knowledge. Understanding is produced through query, acquired by agents involved in query, and is modified and transformed by changes in query over time. Query is therefore the basis of all learning and all discovery, at every stage of cognitive development, at the frontiers of human knowledge and in the elementary classroom. The specific queries undertaken vary, of course, depending on circumstances and conditions. But the general pattern, the emphasis on invention, insight, and discovery, is essential in every cognitive undertaking.[7]

Insight and query are closely related: query is guided by insight and depends on it for its transcendent and inventive powers; insight can be methodically guided and controlled only by query. The two are linked by the concept of *perspective,* since understanding is always relative to a sphere of relations which makes query intelligible, and insight involves transcendence from presented data to a relational context that gives them structure, intelligibility, and meaning. Our cognitive abilities — interpretation, understanding, and affirmation — depend on our being able to inhabit the organizing perspectives which make our surroundings intelligible. Insight is the power that enables us to respond to a perspective cognitively, to make valid judgments relative to that perspective; query is the means whereby we create new cognitive perspectives out of old ones. Both of them depend on our capacity to enter into and share perspectives with others, in whole or in part.

Further details of the theory of insight and query will be developed in Part III. We may return here to the opposition of facts and theories which underlies much of the epistemological discussion above. This opposition is closely related to the distinction between two primary modes of instruction: the acquisition of facts to which cognitive abilities of organization, systematization, and association are later applied; and the development of insights related to familiar subject matters and materials through ongoing query. The status of facts in the epistemological views discussed above is crucial: if facts are essentially independent of theories and paradigms, and define the justificatory basis for such theories, then they supply grounds for cognitive claims that do not vary with context and perspective. If facts are essentially language- and theory-dependent, however, there appears to be an extreme relativism that undermines most claims to validity and truth. Analogously, if facts are distinct from insight and understanding, then they may be acquired in preliminary phases of instruction by memorization and repetition, and may form the materials of later insights. On the other hand, if facts are largely unintelligible except as understood, pervaded by insight, then they appear to have no status at all, varying with different forms of conception.

I am arguing that there are no facts independent of insight and understanding, that these are necessary to the constitution of facts as such. In a stronger sense, I hold that the unqualified statement that a given proposition is a fact is always false or misleading. I must therefore distinguish my position from the relativism that dissipates all truth, renders all objectivity mere interpretation, and would, if taken literally, transform science into a set of merely interesting opinions.

The claim that facts are dependent on interpretation, understanding, and insight seems to suggest that there are no facts, only opinions. And there is some truth to this conclusion, though we cannot accept it as it stands. The statement "there are no facts" cannot be true without being false. However, consider instead "there are no unqualified facts". No statement without qualification is true—and the range of relevant qualifications is inexhaustible.

The claim that there are only interpretations, that no truths are ever completely grounded on established evidence, is also true, though modestly rather than sceptically. We are emphasizing the conditions of query, the perspective which understanding requires. A statement is a mere formula until interpreted *in some context* or *under some conditions,* relative to some perspective. It is the perspective, context, or conditions which, only tacitly acknowledged, make the formula of significance.

While interpretations are functions of conditions and perspectives, not all interpretations are equally valid for any given perspective or for all established perspectives. Interpretations may fail for many reasons and in many applications. The crucial point is that many different applications, conditions, and perspectives are relevant to the validity of every cognitive claim. Scientific knowledge consists in propositions but also in the insights and skills necessary to the reliable and effective application of such propositions in diverse contexts. A mere assertion or "fact" is nothing in itself, even treacherous and misleading. A fact is to be understood only through an act of mind that transcends it and interprets it, in a comprehension of its usefulness and also of its limitations, relative to some or many perspectives. "The sum of the angles of a triangle is 180°" is no fact in itself: it is false both for triangles on the surface of the earth and for large triangles whose sides are the paths of rays of light. It is reasonable to hold that only under an interpretation is it meaningful. It does not follow, however, that uninterpreted, statements are meaningless. For there would then be two kinds of meaninglessness: that under an interpretation, and that in the absence of any interpretation. Rather, interpretation and insight are implicit in whatever is taken to be meaningful. It is more correct to say that a mere sequence of symbols or sounds is no truth, no statement, not even a candidate for meaning, except under an interpretation; and that such an interpretation defines the limitations as well as the applicability of the given statement. But it can never do so completely; and therefore, all statement-making is limited and fallible. Equivalently, we may emphasize the insight necessary to transform a string of symbols into a claim, the insight that produces understanding. Without insight, there is no meaning, no understanding, no knowledge.

How then are we to understand the notion of "facts"? It is

certainly no mere bias that facts are the basis of the physical sciences. On the other hand, nothing is more stultifying than facts which must be accepted without the prospect of a reinterpretation that reconstitutes them. The insight which makes it possible to understand a fact is a capacity which places it in a systematic relationship with other truths, a fact by virtue of this interrelationship. A fact in a scientific experiment is one by virtue of the laws and principles which govern the experiment. It follows that facts may be defined by the roles they play—roles defined by an indefinite plurality of considerations related to both the social and theoretical conditions of the system and the indefinite applicability of scientific theories and laws.

Three distinctions together seem to me to uniquely characterize facts as we understand them in the empirical sciences as well as in more colloquial contexts of everyday experience. The characterization seems to me to avoid scepticism, since facts are defined in terms of the procedures which provide whatever security we can give to truths we accept. However, the approach lays paramount emphasis on the *interpretive* or *visionary* aspect of all factual truth. Facts are facts because of the roles they play. We understand them as facts only in terms of the spheres, systems, and activities in which they function. This understanding is given by what I have called "insight". It follows that the teaching of facts alone, by memorization or rote, is not merely limited or stultifying—it is impossible. I will explain the consequences of this in a moment.

1) In any interpretation, some principles or truths, methods or viewpoints, are presupposed and constitute it. These are not always susceptible to precise formulation, but they are essential nevertheless. Philosophical analysis is often an attempt to embody in a relatively precise formulation the vague principles definitive of an interpretation or activity. Thus, Socrates assumes that justice is a part of virtue, that a craft is defined by standards of excellence inherent in the activity, not in the personal interests of the craftsman, and so forth. The principles appealed to, which define the arguments and proofs offered, are the truths I have in mind. Descartes argues that embodied within his method of syste-

matic doubt is at least one principle which cannot itself be doubted: that every inquiry contains an investigator undertaking the inquiry. Such truths I shall call "constitutive" truths, constitutive of the activities involved. They are the truths "taken for granted" in the activity which employs them.

This notion of "constitutiveness" is fundamental to any understanding of cognitive activities.[8] I have emphasized *truths* constitutive of an activity or point of view: I mean to indicate that such truths are based on evidence and are the conclusions of arguments. They may be distinguished from methodological and formal principles which condition cognitive activities but which are not commonly thought of as true, and especially distinguished from rules, such as the rules of chess, which constitute the game, but which are not true or false.[9] I mentioned above that these constitutive truths, principles, or rules are often imprecisely formulated. It may be more correct to say that they are sometimes not formulated at all, known but unattended to—as are the principles of deep structure of language, the similarities that constitute many structuralist theories. Involved here is a principle fundamental to the theory of insight: that all explicit knowledge is grounded on an unformulated—even to some extent unformulatable—knowledge implicit as the constitutive basis for what can be formulated explicitly. In the case of facts, however, we are usually dealing with explicitly known and formulated truths.

2) Interpretations are not separate and distinct, but form interrelated families. Discoveries from one branch of science are often taken over into other disciplines and sciences with great fruitfulness. Some truths which are essential to a given interpretation are essential also to other interpretations, and may be constitutive in several relatively distinct types of interpretation. Thus, the principle that a truth inhabits a domain of public judgment, even of universal assent, applies equally well to the empirical sciences and to ethics, though the principles accepted in each appear to rest on a completely different foundation. Truths constitutive among many different modes of interpretation I call "truths of wide range". Width of range is a relative notion, and principles are not easily comparable with

respect to width. Nevertheless, where interpretations are inter-related, their interrelationship is due to a common family of truths constitutive of many of them.

3) Some interpretations are essentially static, and engage no methods of activity or investigation. Some interpretations, however, possess their character because of the methods in which they arise. Of these methods, some are methods in which, in an extended scene, questions are posed and answered. Thus, there are interpretations which are both methodic and interrogative. We are approaching query, with its emphasis on invention and validation. Clearly the sciences utilize such methods, for they are forms of query, and all scientific interpretations satisfy the definition I am proposing. But philosophy, law, mathematics, and art are also interrogative and methodic: they are also forms of query. We need, then, a further distinction — between methods which have well-formulated observations among their constitutive truths, and methods which do not such as mathematics. The former methods I will call "empirical". It is a commonplace to distinguish *a priori* logical principles constitutive of mathematics and other formal systems from the "facts" which rest on an empirical foundation in the physical sciences.

We may note here Quine's argument that no sharp distinction between empirical and formal, synthetic and analytic truths can be maintained, since we can always shift from one set of analytic truths to another, keeping the effective applicability of our theory intact.[10] From the point of view involved here, such a weakening of the line between analytic and synthetic truths is an indication that facts are even less independent of theoretical considerations and conditions than I have suggested so far. Still, the identification of a truth as a fact does suggest that it is susceptible to confirmation and disconfirmation, however indirectly, by the collection of evidence.

I propose, then, to define facts as truths which satisfy the three conditions I have set forth: *a fact is a truth of wide range, constitutive among many modes of interpretation which are methodic, interrogative, and empirical.* Observations are not facts until they have been assimilated into an interpretation.

They are not even observations. A witness of a seance, subjected to ghostly phenomena, has no "facts" to offer except within a purely sensory interpretation of raps, clanks, and rattles. Sensory descriptions constitute a common mode of interpretation for a trained observer—constitute it because the entire interpretation is rendered dubious if an observer's memory or ability to describe the phenomena is challenged. When we are at a loss to give a complex, inferential interpretation, we often fall back on descriptions of what we saw and heard, in a terminology which we hope is without dubious interpretive components. "The woman entered the box; the magician passed a cloth in front of her; she vanished." Perhaps it wasn't a box; perhaps it wasn't a mere cloth; perhaps she only seemed to vanish due to some trick with mirrors, but was there all the time. Such a description is highly interpretive, but it is often accepted as a minimal account from which inferences will proceed. In this sense, perceptual descriptions constitute a mode of interpretation and a highly fallible and important one. In highly abnormal circumstances, where new phenomena or strong emotions are involved, we may rightly suspect all our established methods of interpretation, casting about as best we can for an alternative mode.

It does not follow from the definition that there are only a few facts. The sciences, in themselves and as they inform common-sense experience, exhibit a growing set of truths with the properties I have defined. Moreover, connected with every event are determinants which may be ascertained within some interpretations to be facts. These reports of witnesses and testimony of experts are among our most important sources of facts. Even to cast them into doubt on the whole—as against registering doubt toward some of them—is unthinkable. The acknowledgment that political considerations color all our judgments about people in society does not entail that there can be no social facts, but that they are particularly complex and deceitful, and we must check them against each other recurrently and unceasingly. The denial that there are facts is a denial of the validity of the modes of query which work with facts and which are constituted by them. We may at best suggest different ways of arriving at, justifying, or employing facts—different forms of query appropriate within a field of knowledge. We cannot reject facts entirely and maintain the viability of cognitive thought in such a field.

When people lack insight into the domains of interpretation which are constituted by facts, or are suspicious of such insight, they may challenge the legitimacy of those facts. They repudiate them on the grounds that all facts possess intrinsic limitations. They fail to see that the limitations which are provided by contexts of interpretation are essential to the very nature of facts. All knowledge transcends its conditions and foundations — to the perspectives and interpretations that give it meaning and to contexts and applications which it only promises to meet. Because there are no "mere" or unqualified facts, insight into a wide domain of relations is essential to any understanding of facts as such.

It follows that memorization is no pathway to understanding facts, nor even to grasping that they are facts. The conception of a preparatory stage in learning in which facts are acquired prior to the formation of insights is fundamentally in error. Only through understanding can a fact be apprehended as a fact; and insight is necessary to such understanding. I will now examine this principle in relationship to university education and the so-called "disciplines" or branches of knowledge. Every branch of learning, I have argued, is permeated by important forms of insight and understanding. The fundamental questions for education are just how learning is constituted by insight and how such insight is to be engendered in a student who does not possess it.

CHAPTER 6

Discipline

The concept of a discipline appears to have three distinct but related meanings. The primary meaning is that of a branch of knowledge, a domain of cognitive activity. Here there is no intrinsic separation of learning and discovery, but joint participation by teachers and students in a field of knowledge. Yet the word is closely related to the notion of disciple, one who follows a master's teachings. The influence of the latter meaning on the first is subtle but effective, suggesting that a branch of knowledge consists of leaders and followers. Misleading as this notion is, however, it is far outclassed by the perniciousness of the third meaning: that of proper conduct and regulation. I believe that the latter two meanings too often pervade our conception of understanding in a discipline, turning us away from insight to diligence, from understanding to repetition, and emphasizing regulation rather than invention.

The modern meanings of "discipline" can be found in any dictionary of the English language. Most of the listings refer to *control and regulation* and *formation of character.* Here education is primarily moral, and a corresponding sense of discipline is frequently carried over into the branches of knowledge within a university. It is sometimes argued, for example, that the study of foreign languages is beneficial to character, that mathematics benefits the mind.

In practice, college instruction is closely related to the

regulation of character and thought. College students are expected to sit quietly in their hardback seats while the lecturer drones on, and to attend without letting their attention stray; to file conscientiously from one end of the campus to the other in a ten-minute break between classes; to redirect their attention and to attend equally carefully to another lecture having no connection with the first; to prepare individually for common examinations; and so forth. We must consider the institutional conditions for such expectations, which are largely generated by problems of organization and economy, not alone by a concern for teaching and learning. Nevertheless, the effect of such practices is to make university education primarily a place of discipline in the sense of regulation and rule. In practice, the branches of learning appear to be far more effective means of control and of shaping character than inspirations to discovery or the love of wisdom.

The perniciousness of the conception of education as discipline is exacerbated by its partial truth. Learning is indeed hard work, to be accomplished only through dedication and effort. Yet to emphasize the effort is to make diligence the primary factor. Far more important is the difficulty of attaining a novel insight, a new way of looking at the world, which may involve a radical transformation in one's understanding of things. Commitment, authority, and effort must be accompanied by detachment, insight, and freedom if invention and understanding are to be attained.[11]

I have introduced the notion of insight to resolve the paradox of learning and to make sense of the cognitive and inventive powers of the mind. The theory of insight will be developed in the next chapter. In the rest of this chapter I will argue that many of the problems of university education today can be interpreted as institutional forms taken by the university in trying to meet the constraints of the paradox of learning. Although most of my discussion will specifically address the American system of higher education, I will comment briefly on the English honors system. It is a system of higher learning in which insight and invention are of paramount importance; even so, the paradox of learning has a subtly pernicious influence upon it and is almost inescapable.

The paradox returns wherever an elitist emphasis on originality effectively excludes students who are thought capable only of memorization and repetition. There can be no learning without original insights.

Even the university's function as a conservative social force, discriminating between those who will be accepted into the mainstream and those who will not, reflects a pessimistic view of learning in the way those who fail are typically regarded. Most internal and external influences on the contemporary university as an educational institution direct it toward repetition, standardization, and regulation, and away from invention, insight, and diversity. The capacity of the mind to gain novel insights despite these influences is testimony once again to its inventive cognitive powers.

Institutional Constraints

Though usually non-profit and untaxed, and frequently subsidized, universities are subject to important economic constraints. These may be divided into two for convenience, though they overlap: constraints imposed on educational activities in the name of economy; and constraints imposed by the university's relationship to the outside world as a social institution. I will begin with the second of these, the less important for our purposes.

Outside Influences

In some fashion a university must obtain the resources to pursue its activities, both in education and research. Typically, there are but four sources for operating funds: alumni, business operations, tuition, and the government. Each of these compromises the university's educational activities in important ways. The classic pressures from alumni are biased toward support for medical, engineering, business, and law schools. The effect is to emphasize the practically useful studies whose mastery will make one a more effective economic agent. Skills become the paradigm of university education. Now all understanding depends on insight, including the application of useful skills. However, professional and vocational instruction tend to emphasize predefined standards of performance on which certification rests. That first class physicians, lawyers, and computer programmers must be inventive and imaginative is taken for granted, but separated from the standards of professional certification. The paradox of learning is greatly exacerbated.

Business operations do not affect classroom activities in so direct a way, but they nevertheless influence them subtly through constraints exerted on the faculty. Boards of trustees are usually businessmen who are responsible for managing the financial affairs of the university as effectively as possible. They also control the university, appoint the president, and define the rules and regulations of most private institutions. Faculty as well as students are subject to such regulations and learn to conform without jeopardizing their positions or salaries. A man who conforms in one area of his life easily learns to do so elsewhere.

The status of the university as an economic institution subject to governmental regulation and community pressures tends to make boards of trustees highly conservative not only in their investment policies and relations with their employees, but relative to prevailing political controversies. Universities are so vulnerable to external political forces, and are so dependent on political and economic support from outside groups, that they must avoid political controversies that would jeopardize their economic stability. Inevitably, academic disciplines are purged of controversy as well, and de-politicized. But since moral and political issues are central in many fields — the social sciences in particular — the objectification of these disciplines deprives them of their power. Whether there can be viable social theories which are morally and politically neutral is a controversial and difficult question. It can only be influenced perniciously by institutional and economic considerations that promote an ostensibly neutral stance for external reasons.

Major threats today stem from the need for tuition and govern- ment support. The effect of tuition is more subtle not only in private universities which must be self-supporting, but also in publicly-supported universities insofar as they face the problem of providing advanced education for students who cannot afford it. Consider first the private university, which pays an established professor $35,000 a year, and charges its students $6,000 for tuition, not including living expenses, room or board. Surely a single professor could educate ten students for a year with lectures, small discussions, and private tutorials, educating them far better than they are being educated now, and still have time left for personal studies since there would be virtually no administrative responsibilities. We are told that tuition covers no more than one-third of the expenses of a university. Something is wrong with such an institution if it does not achieve economies of scale.

Tuition covers only one-third of the expenses of the university, while it comprises at most one-half of the expenses the student must pay. The concatenation of these two facts make it almost impossible for a truly poor student to attend a prestigious private university. Such universities seek to compensate by charging a very high tuition to those who can afford it and granting relatively large scholarships to very poor students. However, since tuition covers but a small portion of the total cost of the educational system, such support can be given to but a very small percentage of students, even where relatively large endowments are available. On the other hand, universities supported by public funds do not give large scholarships, though they charge relatively low tuition fees.

Severe inequities are generated by these economic realities, though they are not as scandalous as other inequities which will be considered later. I am concerned here with implications for learning and the classroom. Economic conditions tend to produce uniformity and homogeneity. Inevitably, a standard vision of the world as well as of understanding is generated. Diversity and imagination are constrained by such homogeneity, and the range of controversies is severely confined.

The most treacherous influence on university education is governmental support. Its effects on the structure of the university are well known. Nevertheless, there is no question that the institutional character of colleges and universities must make them both accountable to the public and responsive to social needs. I am not disputing the right of government agencies to influence educational policies through expenditures nor to demand that institutions supported in part by public funds fulfill public policies. Yet there is a covert and subtle influence such expectations impose on university activities that runs counter to the cognitive impulses inherent in them. Relationships between fields of knowledge are distorted, and fields with the most obvious immediate applications are given theoretical support. Common standards of performance are frequently imposed where controversy and inventiveness may be more appropriate.

Far more important, however, is a uniformity of expectation derived almost typically from legislative and political consider- ations. One effect of a problem-solving approach to complex social and political issues is a standardization and homogeniz- ation of structure imposed on a plurality of diverse institutions. An example has been the development of a single, relatively uniform model of a university. Generally speaking, major universities in the United States today, especially where supported by public funds, are identical or strive toward an identical model. There is but a slight plurality of differing conceptions of education and of ways to accomplish it. The student has little choice, within his own economic constraints, of educational possibilities.

The most powerful effect of government support resides in its effective separation of research and teaching since people who can contribute to government projects are directly supported without teaching responsibilities. Contributing to this as well is the emphasis on research and publication as avenues to profes- sional advancement. Where a domain of knowledge separates discovery and learning, though in all important respects they are identical, then the learning which is left to the classroom becomes an empty chore. The university is either a repository of items of knowledge, like a library, which can be withdrawn routinely, or it seeks further discoveries which can be realized only through understanding. Remove the insight essential to discovery from teaching and learning, and there is left only the drudgery of accu- mulated facts and techniques.

The economic realities I have mentioned move the university toward limited vision, either in promoting uniformity or in separating vision from performance. But as vision becomes inhibited, subject matters remain, to be acquired by diligence and labor, by work without love, effort without the guidance of insight. The economic pressures upon higher education lead to the substitution of disciplines for understanding. In part, this is inherent in the conception of a discipline as a field of instruction rather than a branch of knowledge. The paradox of learning is unresolvable once we propose an authority for whom the instruction of ignorant students and the activities of research and discovery are entirely disconnected in both theory and practice. The theory of insight entails that discovery and learning are identical in principle, though they may play different roles for different persons. The critical point is that "mere" teaching, for purposes other than for discovery, is devoid of vision and leads to the replacement of insight by drudgery and repetition.

Internal Economic Limitations

To this point we have considered only the sources of the university's operating funds and the aims imposed by them. Domains of knowledge become disciplinary in the worst sense when their aims are imposed on them from without and when their unique modes of vision are subordinated to external constraints. There are, however, economic imperatives within the university itself, generated by the reality that there is never enough money to do everything that has to be done. This is a pervasive condition of mankind. Within the university, however, economic limitations tend to replace vision by organized effort and support the transition from learning to discipline.

We may consider some of the specific ways in which economic conditions affect practices within the university. Most obvious is the university's expansion over the past few decades. Complex networks of public instruction have been developed. Separate institutions are assigned distinct functions in the system according to a master plan evolved by a central board which is located on no campus and which is directly concerned with the special needs and prerogatives of no particular institution. A continual tension emerges between the constraints imposed centrally according to the over-all plan and the autonomy of members of the system.

Two consequences follow from this situation; together they conspire in a single direction. Of the funds allocated to a single institution by the central board or legislature, a sizable portion is earmarked for programs mandated by the board and imposed without remedy on the local institution. The energies of the local institution are diverted, and resources which might be put into the programs of its special competence are spent elsewhere. This is true even where local autonomy is encouraged. In addition, aims determined according to an over-all plan promote uniformity among the members of the system. The result is a consumer conception of education, meeting all needs and challenging none. Television networks tell us that the consumer determines programming by numbers alone. Quality fails when an institution seeks to satisfy everyone without controversy and to generate no challenges. Every university must have the same departments and the same courses, to serve the same students indistinguishably. Bureaucratic conformity replaces a plurality of visions, a conformity without sense or aim except that of efficiency.

Systems of public higher education make a distinction among institutions at different levels: junior colleges, four-year colleges, and universities. Such a distinction is required by economic conditions, for instruction in universities is far more costly than at junior colleges. Virtually all the schools on the same level are stamped out of the same mold, but there is modest plurality of differing levels and educational aims. Unfortunately, the social effects of this distinction are egregious. In general, students who attend universities are superior students. In addition, they possess distinct economic advantages by virtue of their university education. The result is that the poor are not prepared effectively for university education, and remain disadvantaged. The effect of higher education in perpetuating class differences is quite strong. It is a natural consequence of a uniform system of public instruction that is supposed to meet the differing needs of diverse kinds of students.

Within the university, the scarcity of economic resources, coupled with the trend toward providing higher education for all, promotes great growth and complexity, with all the ugliness leviathans seem to require. Some of the imperatives at work here arise from quite laudable motives. The conception of man as a creature who never ceases to learn is humane and enlightened. The opening of facilities of higher education to everyone is the greatest single factor in the implementation of equal opportunity.[12] Unfortunately, the means for accommodating increasing numbers of students has been the development of uniform institutions of gigantic size, in which conformity and identity replace plurality.

Within a single university the uniform expectations imposed from without promote a plurality of functions. Such a bureaucracy is self-sustaining, since a complex institution requires human beings trained in its management whose success is measured by the size and complexity of the institution they manage. This complexity of functions leads still further in the direction of uniformity, since several institutions, each of which requires a balanced relationship among similar elements and activities, tend to find common solutions. Uniformity when coupled with gigantic size breeds further uniformity. Bureaucracy breeds further bureaucracy. The result is a system without personal character, containing no sense of itself except a geographical location, an assemblage of distinct activities and functions without discernible interconnection. In short, the university has become a multiversity, a bureaucracy with no vision of its aims or nature.[13]

The result is that the administration and faculty can find no consensus as to the function of their university, nor even several well-defined but distinction conceptions or visions. No wonder that students have none. The routine of separate activities replaces a sense of purpose and a vision of achievement. Courses become not means to learning, at least in a comprehensive sense, but activities complete in themselves: reading assigned texts, writing assigned papers, answering assigned questions. No vision rules over these separate activities, and they remain disconnected and meaningless. This explains the readiness of some students to abandon the writing of papers, others to abandon examinations, still others even to stop reading. Since no intrinsic aim or insight presides over these activities, a student might as well engage in those which please him the most. These activities are seen as scholastic or academic devices, rather than as activities intrinsic to a domain of understanding.

I will argue that the *intellectual* organization of the contemporary university supports the same trends, and would probably do so effectively without support from economic conditions. What is dismaying is how economic conditions and intellectual principles work together. Other consequences of the scarcity of economic resources in growing institutions support the same trends — away from inspiration and vision, and toward stereotyped disciplines, senseless activities, conformity and uniformity in intellectual enterprises. Consider just a few:

Class size

It is a universal trend, seemingly without exception, that classes grow in size. It follows from clear economic imperatives, since the more students a given teacher handles, the lower the cost per student of the teacher's salary.

Assistant teachers

An alternative, either in place of or a complement to increasing class size, is the use of graduate students as teachers in under-graduate classes. I have no criticisms to offer of the use of such teachers in small classes of their own, provided they are qualified for such work. Sometimes such teachers bring an enthusiasm and concern to their students which experienced teachers may lack. The dangers are that a graduate student may lack an over-all conception of his field, and that he may be distracted from his teaching by his responsibilities as a student. Both of these would lead him to substitute repetition for insight. The more important trend is toward larger classes in which graduate students are used as assistant teachers. They are often the only teachers whom beginning undergraduates have an opportunity to speak to directly. Far more important, the difficulties of generating a strong sense of order and vision in a class taught by a multiplicity of teachers, only some of whom are very experienced, are insuperable.

Instructional media

Television and other technological devices stand in a complementary relationship to the trend toward larger classes. Once classes have grown sufficiently in size, television and film become natural aids. In return, they involve so large a capital investment as to be prohibitive unless savings are effected in instruction. Thus, if television is valuable for some applications, it will lead to larger classes; while if larger classes are required, television seems naturally entailed. Computer-assisted forms of instruction are similar devices with similar results.

Standardized examinations

The most arduous and time-consuming aspect of instruction is frequently not the actual teaching but the grading of examinations and papers. No methods of cutting costs can be effective unless the time involved in grading examinations is reduced as well. The obvious step is that of standardization: examinations graded by computer or by key. This step is supported further by the view that such examinations are more "objective", more legitimate, providing clearly demarcated right or wrong answers. I will not discuss this view here except to note that it is a feature of the trend toward institutionalized mediocrity in university education discussed below, and that it is entirely incompatible with the development of insight and understanding.

All of the trends noted generate the same result: less contact during the instructional process between the teacher and the student in any but predetermined ways. The student possesses little power to guide the direction of his learning. In a small class, instruction is in part a matter of mutual effort in which the teacher adapts both his questions and his presentation to the students' evinced interests and insights. In such a class, time can be given both to the slower student who needs further explanation and to the idiosyncratic student whose brilliant insights can be followed with value to everyone. It is irrelevant that many small classes possess none of the flexibility just described. A student in a class of fifteen students senses his own power within the class (as well as his responsibilities) and the value of his insights. In a small class, insights and divergent points of view are an important part of the process of learning.

The trend to larger classes inevitably brings with it greater regimentation and predetermination. The lectures must be prepared in advance. The students may listen or not as they choose, but they may not interfere with the course of the lecture nor direct it in any way. A large class can in principle open a space for individual initiative and insight. However, coupled with the other trends involving assistant teachers and standardized examinations, there is little opportunity for a student to develop the powers sought. Instructional activities become ends in themselves, activities undertaken for no larger purpose and directed to no transformation of vision.

I have discussed to this point only the economic factors which contribute to the transformation of studies within the university into disciplines in the colloquial sense of regimentation, labor, and effort. There are two other factors that push the university in the same directions.

Specialization

If the university is a repository of knowledge, then contemporary knowledge is stacked in separate bins in the warehouse, cross-filed in the library index, but without discernible overlap among disciplines. We are in an era of a new scholasticism, in which the burning issues which fill the journals and make the professional reputations of experts are unintelligible not only to everyone outside the field, but even within the same general discipline. University professors become expert in their particular period, age, milieu, or problem area, and only peripherally touch on other fields or periods. Even where interdisciplinary effort is encouraged, it is thought of as an educational device, useful in stimulating the thinking of the young and relatively ignorant student, and valuable only because of his ignorance. A specialist may with considerable effort learn to teach in an interdisciplinary fashion, but he is certainly not expected to be able to make original contributions of a comprehensive nature. (Geniuses are exempted from this condition, but that is the point of the discussion which will follow.) Most specialists feel incompetent even to touch superficially on disciplines not their own, and most general education programs which were developed in the 1930's and 40's were abandoned in the 1960's and 70's. As the pendulum swings back again in the 1980's, new general education proposals are faced with the difficulty that interdisciplinary programs cannot be staffed by persons who are also expected to engage in highly specialized research.

The specialists who abhor all forms of general education at least have the virtue of consistency, though they find themselves defending a position that has no defense. If the university is comprised of people who possess no unifying vision or comprehensive synthesis of human knowledge, then it is hypocritical, misleading, and superficial to attempt to teach college courses as if such a synthesis were possible and to define a core curriculum fit for all students. Insofar as we are honest, we will portray a university education as what it is, specialized and narrow in its focus. Insofar as our aim in higher education is the development of the next generation of researchers, we must develop specialists only.

It is worth pointing out that extreme specialization is not intrinsic to studies such as literature, philosophy, anthropology, history, or sociology. The paradigms of specialization seem to be drawn from two polar extremes: the physical sciences and classics. In the case of physics, the domain of knowledge has expanded so rapidly, research has required such precision and endurance, that specialization is unavoidable. In classical studies, the general conclusions have been known for hundreds of years, and original research requires the utmost effort to uncover hitherto obscured details. Even in these two cases, there is a larger enterprise — theoretical science in the one case, the critical analysis of the great ancient works in the other—which would seem to be the touchstone of success and value even for specialized research. Such larger enterprises cannot be narrowly specialized and still possess great value.

Specialization has two dimensions which are distinguishable, yet which usually go hand in hand. These are a *narrowness* of focus on problems of original research, and the *distinctness* of the activities engaged in and problems defined. Narrowness is not evil in itself, though like all good things it can be overdone. Scholarship calls for the weeding out of extraneous elements. A problem must be whittled down to size before it can be solved. Specialization becomes vicious when it promotes distinctness to an extreme, and leads to specialties with no discernible overlap, which are pursued in isolation from each other, and which do not inform and revitalize each other. The sciences, though the sources of the paradigm of specialization, constantly look for new ways of conceiving problems, of defining new theoretical approaches, of unifying separate branches. But in the social sciences and especially the humanities, specialization leads to disconnection and frequently to stultification.

Many students sense the limitations of arbitrarily separated subject matters. They wonder why it is not possible to study *man* as a living organism, culturally and intellectually, rather than in separate disciplines, why we are not concerned with all the arts and their interconnections. By a strange irony, they overlook an important argument *for* specialization: that we cannot study man in general without studying him in detail; that the ways in which different arts are similar may be considerably less important than the ways in which they are unique. The students protest that narrowness leads to sterility; the reply is that no one can grasp the great topics without understanding some of the small ones. Nevertheless, though students may be asking for something impossible to achieve in the classroom, they possess a devastating insight. That is, that narrow specialties are valuable only as they inform each other ultimately. Narrow studies of man must lead to a larger comprehension of humanity or they are wasted. A comprehensive vision must both guide and be the outcome of narrow investigations if they are to be valuable. Important research is always guided by a larger sense of issues and purposes, grounded at best in a comprehensive and powerful theory. Insight into connections and disconnections, similarities and differences, is essential to all understanding. Sheer separation is antithetic to insight.

If research calls for interpenetrating visions, then students are correct to demand that the classroom embody such interpenetration also, at least to the extent that it is possible to do so. Otherwise we separate discovery from learning, and leave only labor and effort behind. In a classroom, the students make discoveries and must do so if they are to learn. But if these discoveries are merely make-believe; if the classroom pretends to discovery when the teacher really knows everything that can happen, then learning will be stunted and make-believe. The student will learn what the teacher already knows. Perhaps he will come to see something in a new way. Perhaps not. Without emphasis on his discoveries, we leave his most important learning to chance. Traditionally, the physical sciences have emphasized the importance of laboratory work in teaching science to nonscientists. But they have developed laboratory courses in which routine activities lead only to results which could be gathered from any textbook. Discovery is eliminated yet students are asked to pretend they may discover something new. In the last few years, laboratories have largely been abandoned as too expensive and unsuccessful. That is a shame, for in principle laboratory work in the sciences is a great aid to understanding. However, if students are to learn what experimentation involves, then put them in a laboratory for a semester or a year and let them design their own experiments — with guidance — and make their own discoveries. If this is impossible, then abandon the attempt to teach experimental method to nonscientists.

The primary argument in favor of specialization in the university, both in research and in education, is that knowledge has grown so rapidly that no single person can master it all — as if anyone in ancient Greece or in Leonardo's time knew everything that was to be known. The force of this argument is considerable when addressed to the prospect of a comprehensive synthesis of all human knowledge in a total system. However, an all-encompassing synthesis is not the only alternative to extreme specialization. Another alternative is that of *epistemic pluralism*. No one may be able to master all of human knowledge, but it is possible to be competent in several related fields, if not master of more than one or two of them. We emphasize here a plurality of insights and visions which inform each other, though each is in itself limited. We accept narrowness, but locate it within a context of multiplicity and interconnection. Most of all, we respect the distinctness of different specializations, aiming not to fuse them together or to organize them systematically, but to bring different specialties to bear on each other at their boundaries while preserving their singular characteristics.

Institutionalized Mediocrity

The intellectual progress of humanity until this century has rested upon the contributions of relatively few human beings of transcendent abilities and achievements. Such persons stand to ordinary human beings of lesser gifts as giants, awesome figures of incredible gifts and overpowering vision. One of the regrettable consequences of institutional democracy is a repudiation of innate superiority and the leveling of eminence. The examples which represent the human mind in action are far too often ordinary people with routine accomplishments, effectively minimizing the inventiveness and transcendence of the mind which are its salient characteristics.

All bureaucracies, especially as they become more uniform and enveloping, encourage conformity. A bureaucracy with genuine power — such as the federal government — seeks to mask its police and avoid the use of naked force. A university, possessing no brute force, is even more vulnerable to turmoil. Conformity to the system, at least to its practices and government, is imperative. But we cannot expect conformity and uniformity in style of life without conformity as well in thought and vision. A person who views intellectual responsibility as that of permanent challenge to entrenched powers has no place in the contemporary university.

A modern version of Socrates or Spinoza would be no more welcome today than in their own bureaucracies.

In addition, the paradigm of the natural sciences has permeated all phases of the university. In the sciences, every person has a place and with diligent effort can make a contribution to his field, a genuine contribution which no one else has made before. Science is the intellectual activity whose performance most easily transforms intellectual labor into value. Hard work has a clear worth. Properly conceived, any experiment can be said to solve a problem, thus to be successful and valuable. While people of great vision are as important in science as in any other domain of knowledge, and are the source of its major advances in knowledge, there is a vital role played by scientists of modest vision.

Other fields are not like the sciences in this respect.[14] A modest and unassuming novel is worth little beyond the pleasures of the moment. A mediocre painter makes no contributions to our artistic sensibilities. A mediocre philosopher is no philosopher at all—though we hope he may become a good teacher of philosophy (if someone without important philosophic insights can be a good teacher of philosophy). Unfortunately, scientific research has become paradigmatic of research in all fields of knowledge. Even the word "research" is anomalous for original work in the humanities. Where uniqueness of interpretation is primary—as in philosophy or literary criticism—people do not engage in research whatever they do and however much they produce. The routine labor which is research has significance only in the laboratory or in the library.

The paradigm of scientific research in the modest, routine sense has become predominant for two reasons. The first I have mentioned: science embodies a genuine conception of valuable work manifested in attention to small details, modest but precise refinements. Analogously, the writing of short articles of an esoteric or specialized character, in a scholarly mode in the current fashion, becomes the paradigm of worthy contribution. In both cases, greatness of vision is the ideal, and is understood to be necessary to the advance of knowledge and understanding, but routine activities become an accepted norm, closely analogous to the way in which memorization and repetition are paradigmatic in most classroom instruction, though inventive and transcendent insights are necessary to any significant understanding.

The second reason for the acceptance of a paradigm of routine research is the need to find a criterion for advancement in the university. A major university must distinguish between its successful and unsuccessful members, between its full professors and its lowly instructors, between those who have made important contributions to intellectual life and those who have not. But if all contributions but for a vanishingly small number are mediocre and of little value, then the typical stratification within a university is unjustifiable and inequitable.

What is required is a relatively straightforward means of publication, with rewards accruing to those who publish most. We therefore find all fields of study pervaded by hundreds of journals in which thousands of articles of between five and ten thousand words appear. There are a few human beings of great insight and understanding. Let us hope their gifts are recognized. But the system of publication for its own sake is the institutionalization of mediocrity. It is designed to allow ordinary human beings of just a little ability to show their gifts—not to make major contributions to knowledge nor to influence the course of intellectual history, but as the basis for their personal advancement.

The result of institutionalized mediocrity is a diminution of vision, an engendering of routine activities, even an explicit rejection of all possibility of greatness. The university becomes a haven for hard work and diligent application. Discipline becomes the most valuable quality a person can have. University professors who do not succeed are not in this context less gifted. They are less disciplined, lazy, do not make proper use of their time. In this context also, it is no wonder that students lack the capacity to be awakened to some vision of the value of learning and yearn for relevance. When wonder and vision are gone, replaced by institutionalized mediocrity, the purpose of an education vanishes with them.

My discussion has been rather general, emphasizing large-scale developments in the American college and university system over the past few decades. No doubt there are individual institutions whose faculty and students escape one or more of the perils I have identified and, committed to the development of insight and understanding, have built a community in which discovery is primary. My point is that the major influences on university activities in the United States tend to militate against insight and vision and tend to foster diligence and repetition, as if the mind could function effectively and cognitively without insight and invention.

An interesting contrast may be made, here, with the English honors system at Oxford and Cambridge. There, unlike the American college system, courses are of minor importance. The three-year program consists of lectures and weekly tutorials, leading to a massive examination at the end with both written and oral parts. In principle, the English system emphasizes mental activity rather than repetition. There is space for the student to pursue his own directions over three years, freed from the confines of routine courses and examinations. There is great emphasis in the tutorials on skills and techniques, on thought and invention. And at the final examinations, repetition and factual knowledge will not earn a first, only a second or third at best.

Many of the institutional influences I have mentioned apply to English universities as well as American ones: they too have economic interests that can be influenced by external factors. Yet there is a long tradition that helps them to resist transitory influences and to establish a larger and more enduring sense of purpose. More important, perhaps, is the movement of intellectual thought throughout the world toward greater specialization and a weakening of conviction as to the nature of higher learning. Tradition can sustain a coherent purpose for only so long a time in the face of genuine intellectual obstacles to synthesis and reconciliation. Moreover, the traditions which imbue Oxford and Cambridge with purpose cannot help but promote homogeneity, a limitation upon the range of cognitive possibilities acceptable at any time. Finally, the emphasis on the tutorial system, where tutors are given lifetime posts from the beginning, does not guarantee the personal encounter by many undergraduates with teachers of vision and accomplishment, certainly not a meeting of minds.

Nevertheless, the major defects of the system lie in its elitism — and this elitism manifests concessions made to the paradox of learning. There is emphasis on insight and creativity but as a measure of quality and of performance, expected only from the very best students. Better minds are more inventive. This is an enormous advance over the view that minds perform their work satisfactorily by sheer repetition. Yet neither system adequately reflects the principle that all understanding requires insight, that invention is a condition and criterion of all knowledge and learning. There are better and worse, broader and narrower, more and less productive insights. The American system tends to postpone an emphasis on insight to graduate school and beyond (except in fields like philosophy and mathematics). The English system emphasizes invention from the beginning — but as a means to stratification. The importance of the examinations makes the norms they foster all the more critical: established facts and skills, techniques and strategies, or adventurousness, variation, uniqueness of point of view. Far too often, standardized facts and techniques are accepted as satisfactory on the assumption that invention is a property only of superior minds.

Neither system, it seems to me, adequately confronts the pervasiveness of invention and insight needed wherever there is cognitive development. This is probably true in part because educational systems tend to foster standardized measures of performance, memorization and repetition, at least for the great majority of students. Students, in their turn, develop the methods and techniques that will help them get ahead, sharing these with each other. Nevertheless, tricks and strategies, facts and rules, all require insight for their acquisition and invention for their application. What is needed is a far closer attention to how insights can be enriched, expanded, directed toward more productive understanding at every level of instruction. The miracle of insight is a pervasive one, not restricted to the greatest achievements, and must be incorporated into every phase of instruction, elementary to university.

CHAPTER 7

Study

If the disciplinary paradigm separates facts from their constitutive insights, and undermines the essential role of vision and invention in understanding, how else should we think of university activities? I have rejected the principle of a unity of all knowledge in a comprehensive synthesis—in theory insofar as different branches of knowledge rest on different constitutive insights; in practice insofar as there is no rational principle whereby the many different branches of learning may be coordinated under a single conception of knowledge. I have replaced so general a synthesis with a principle of activity: learning is discovery, grounded in insight and secured by invention. We need a conception of branches of knowledge based on this principle, for example, that there are many fields of knowledge, interrelated at their boundaries but based on different though interrelated modes of insight. What such a conception emphasizes is that a field of learning is simultaneously a branch of instruction and a field of invention and discovery. It also emphasizes the fundamental importance of insight in constituting a kind of learning.

A similar notion is that of *study,* which includes within a single concept assiduous effort, carefulness, reflective thought, and an organized branch of knowledge. The term "study" addresses in a unified way both the acquisition of learning in instruction and the acquisition of knowledge in inquiry. It reminds us that learning takes place in both education and inquiry, and that the acquisition of knowledge for both the student and the expert is discovery. It brings together the strands which are so sharply separated in the contemporary school—instruction for the novice and discovery by the expert. Both require insight and invention and both are a result of query. In this sense, all cognitive development is produced by query, differing only in the larger human and historical setting for the expert and the novice.

A university is a place of and for study as the aim and object of activities undertaken; as discoveries made and imparted; as diligence devoted to learning. The teacher is knowledgeable because of the studies he has engaged in; the student has just begun his studies and has less deeply penetrated beneath the surface of his mind and the world. A teacher who no longer studies replaces inquiry with instruction and inspiration with diligence. In return, the student who awaits the coming of vision without application lacks a firm conception of study and learning. Study is one of the most complete of human activities —complete in the sense of being simultaneously means and ends. Study is the means to understanding; the understanding realized is simply further participation in the studies involved.

The paradox of learning rests on the assumption that a clear line can be drawn between ignorance and knowledge. If we are ignorant, we cannot tell that we have made a discovery. If we know, we cannot learn. Once a sharp line has been drawn between ignorance and knowledge, then we will inevitably find ourselves on one side of the line or the other, unable to cross over. The solution to the paradox depends on a theory of incomplete and plural but related insights. In order to learn, we must possess a partial vision which enables us to appreciate the truth and value of a discovery, but which is sufficiently incomplete to accommodate further discovery. I will examine this conception of insight in greater detail.

But there is another solution to the paradox through a clearer conception of the relationship between a method of study and its fruits. In a short article which every teacher ought to read, David Hawkins describes the experiments he and his wife performed in teaching science to children.[15] Based on these experiments,

Hawkins promulgates the following principle: "When the mind is evolving the abstractions which will lead to physical comprehension, all of us must cross the line between ignorance and insight many times before we truly understand". This sentence is a trenchant comment on learning and instruction. It states one of the fundamental properties of insight in learning, and makes a compelling criticism of our entire system of formal instruction. How much opportunity is provided in school for crossing and recrossing the line between ignorance and understanding — a crossing which takes place every time in a different place and in a different way? I will return to this subject in the next chapter.

I wish here simply to apply Hawkins' principle to the paradox of learning. In calling both activity and result, instruction and inquiry, by the same word, we emphasize the process in which learning takes place. We make intelligible crossing the line between ignorance and understanding many times. Because of our past studies, we are never quite "ignorant". We traverse back and forth over the subject before us in study as we seek to refine our understanding, clear up some puzzles, and settle our confusions. Suddenly everything falls together and our confusions are dispelled. A moment before we did not understand; now we do. But we have by no means finished our study upon attaining this insight. We must engage in further study to explore its details and to clear up the confusions it generates. New points of view are required; new inadequacies are revealed; new confusions are generated. The process is what we call "study", and in it we move continuously around and through the boundary between ignorance and understanding — a boundary which cannot in fact be said to exist. Rather, there is study at different levels of achievement and sophistication.

It is in study as inseparably both method and result that we find a solution to the paradox of learning.[16] It is in study and learning as inseparably related that the transition is made from ignorance to knowledge. Study here is the interrogative and methodic activity in which knowledge is gained and validation achieved. However, knowledge is not separable from the activity itself but is intelligible only through it. Study produces, grounds, and exhibits knowledge; knowledge is the achievement brought by successful study, realized essentially in further study.

I have identified knowledge with successful query. It is clear that what I am calling "study" here is query: the interrogative and methodic activity of mind in which invention and validation are predominant. The importance of invention I have noted as essential in all forms of insight and understanding. I will now consider briefly the concept of method.[17] I have noted that one of the primary modes of insight is into method: into the organizing principles and activities that constitute a branch of learning.

It is not difficult to show that there is no single method appropriate to any rational enterprise, that multiple methods make novelty essential. Consider the paradigm of a game of chess, chosen because of its strict rules. A game of chess is defined by a set of relatively simple rules. Yet in no sense are intelligence, invention, imagination, and originality to be dispensed with. The rules define the conditions under which intelligence is to be employed, and do so in one set of dimensions precisely. But this is no constraint upon originality—rather, it makes originality more arduous and effective.

The point is that methods are always constituted by submethods and subprocedures. There is a complex interrelationship of procedures, evaluative methods, and conditions of appraisal inherent in any complex method, especially those which involve rationality. The method of playing chess, though defined with unvarying rules, nevertheless accommodates an indefinite range of submethods with an enormous variety of possibilities of action, of attack and defense, of patterns of development. In this way, a rigorously defined method may accommodate a remarkable range of possibilities.

An additional point is that every submethod belongs to more comprehensive methods,[18] though these may be only vaguely conceived at a given time. The methods of the various sciences are submethods of the method of science. Now, it is true that the method of science is not a method with a straightforward and well-defined rules as is a game of chess. But even if it were, it would not follow that routine submethods would be appropriate. To the contrary, insofar as science is a method which calls for intelligence, it requires the invention of particular submethods for the solution to emergent problems. Methodology, which should be the study of methods for producing new and effective methods of understanding, is more often the rationalization of specific methods as they are imposed throughout a discipline. Nothing could be more stultifying. In the classroom, the pretense that a study aims at the grasp of but a single method closes off the fount of possibility inherent in a student's fresh look at older techniques. The flexibility which a plurality of methods affords depends on the uniqueness inherent in the plurality of persons who employ the methods.[19] As methods become monolithic they impose constraints that limit vision, render insight partial, and virtually prohibit major discoveries.

In a study which is methodic, the natural question both for those engaged in inquiry and those learning to master the method is *why* they utilize the method given. To the expert in the field, the answer is clear in some respects—though it is unclear in others. Methods comprise an important kind of implicit knowledge, which must be known and employed but which cannot be satisfactorily formulated and expressed. They also comprise an important class of insights. To the expert, the method can be used effectively to resolve certain kinds of difficulties. His problem is how to adapt the method to the particular difficulties facing him. His expertness consists in his ability to adapt the method when necessary—that is, to change it, modify it, invent new submethods and techniques within it. A student, however, cannot perform such modifications effectively. The paradox of learning returns, for the student must accept the method in order to have grounds for judgment, yet his grounds for accepting the method depend on the method itself. A related conclusion is that both the acquisition of a methodic power and its employment rest on our ability to depart from it. The paradox recurs in the condition that learning is always complemented by unlearning, knowledge by revision.

The resolution to the paradox here rests upon the interrelationship of methods and submethods. A discipline which is but the employment of a single method has no ground within it or without it. It becomes self-justifying, complete in itself, unintelligible in fundamental respects. It forbids the asking of questions which may threaten it. It achieves its status by closing off methodic interrogation. Tolerance of disciplines without criticism from without is equivalent to a repudiation of any concern for their rationality or justification. Lurking within the conventional notion of knowledge for its own sake—the very essence of a university—is a sense of separate and determinate domains of knowledge, each complete in itself and possessing a method complete in itself.

But methods are interrelated. They comprise interconnected spheres with more and less comprehensive methods and sub-methods. Methods resemble each other in certain ways though they are also different in other ways. They are interconnected also insofar as they have common subject matters—as perceptual responses are common to painting, art criticism, psychology, and aesthetics. The plurality of studies establishes a plurality of methods which may be valuable in any specific study as well as a possibility of movement from one method to another.

This interconnection of methods and submethods reflects the interconnection of insights essential to cognitive development. It is only because cognitive powers open up to other cognitive powers that learning and discovery are possible. The continuity I have described among the methods of novice and expert is mirrored by the continuity and interrelatedness of methods and insights in the activities of query within the experience of any individual as he grows in his understanding and mastery of certain methods as they develop out of prior methodic insights. The explanation of how cognitive development is possible rests ultimately on relations among insights and methods, on connections among methods and submethods, on the openness of insights to other insights. Nevertheless, there are no automatic, routine methods for developing novel insights from established insights, for developing new, effective methods from established methods. All such development requires novel insight and discovery. The balance and opposition of these two moments of insight—relatedness and departure—constitute the life of the mind.

The application of inventive and interrogative methods grounded in validation is what I have called query. The methodic power which query provides is the most effective candidate we have for knowledge. We may conclude that query is both the source and test of knowledge, and that we acquire the methods that produce knowledge only through query—only through invention and discovery. What we know is the outcome of an activity, and that activity is the same in principle for teacher and for student. Learning, at every stage and level, is the outcome of query, grounded in the openness of methods and submethods to each other and based on the capacity of the mind to generate novel insights. An adequate theory of learning, then, is a theory of insight grounded in the inventive powers of the mind and in the methodic properties of query.

REFERENCES

1. Rorty, *Philosophy and the Mirror of Nature;* W.V.O. Quine: *Ontological Relativity and Other Essays,* New York, Columbia University Press, 1969; Hans-Georg Gadamer: *Truth and Method,* New York, Seabury, 1975; Jacques Derrida; *Of Grammatology,* Baltimore and London, Johns Hopkins University Press, 1974.
2. Kuhn, *The Structure of Scientific Revolutions.*
3. Rorty, *op. cit.*
4. Derrida, *Of Grammatology;* Martin Heidegger: *On the Way to Language,* New York, Harper and Row, 1971.
5. Both knowledge and being involve a continual interplay of determinateness and indeterminateness, which I have discussed metaphysically in my *Transition to an Ordinal Metaphysics,* Albany, State University of New York Press, 1980, and related to a theory of philosophical mystery in *Philosophical Mysteries,* Albany, State University of New York Press, 1981.
6. Justus Buchler: *Nature and Judgment,* New York, Columbia University Press, 1955, pp. 7, 49. (See also my *Philosophical Mysteries.*)
7. This position is closely related to John Dewey's emphasis on inquiry as the basis of knowledge *(Logic: The Theory of Inquiry,* New York, Holt, 1938), Heidegger's and Gadamer's emphasis on interpretation *(op. cit.),* and Richard Rorty's rejection of foundations in favor of conversation *(Philosophy and the Mirror of Nature).* The problem is to eliminate the sceptical overtones that appear to follow from locating knowledge in the context of human activities.

8. Though constitutive truths define a theory of cognitive activity, they may not be separable from what they constitute. This blurredness of line is analogous to that between knowledge and ignorance: both lines are permeable by query, but every situation in which query occurs presupposes such a line, however blurred it may be.

9. See John Searle: *Speech Acts,* London and New York, Cambridge University Press, 1969.

10. W.V.O. Quine: "Two Dogmas of Empiricism", *Philosophical Review,* Vol. 60, 1950, pp. 20-43; *Ontological Relativity.*

11. See Jerome Bruner: *On Knowing,* Cambridge Massachusetts, Harvard University Press, 1962, esp. pp. 17-30.

12. But see Jencks, *Inequality.*

13. See Clark Kerr: *The Uses of the University,* Cambridge Massachusetts, Harvard University Press, 1964.

14. For a somewhat overstated expression of this characteristic of science, see Jacques Barzun: *Science: The Glorious Entertainment,* New York, Harper & Row, 1964.

15. David Hawkins: "Messing About in Science", *Science and Children,* February 1965; discussed in Holt, *How Children Learn,* pp. 128-135.

16. John Dewey's principle of the continuum of means and ends should be noted here, for the identification of learning and discovery in study is one application of Dewey's principle. See *Theory of Valuation,* Chicago, University of Chicago Press, 1939.

17. See Justus Buchler: *The Concept of Method,* New York, Columbia University Press, 1961.

18. *op. cit.*

19. See here Paul Feyerabend: *Against Method,* Atlantic Highlands, New Jersey, Humanities Press, 1975; Michael Polanyi: *Personal Knowledge,* Chicago, University of Chicago, 1958.

PART III

Vision

CHAPTER 8

Learning

A brief review of the principles established in earlier discussions may be helpful in defining a context for the theory of insight and learning. I have argued that the epistemological issues considered in Plato's *Meno,* particularly those connected with the paradox of learning, have close parallels in the contemporary university. The paradox of learning emerges from the conviction that there is a hard and fast, principled or grounded distinction between knowledge and ignorance. The fundamental issue is how knowledge can emerge from essentially repetitive means, how an untutored infant can develop into a knowledgeable adult, how a transition can be made from instructional procedures that are essentially reproductive and authoritarian to grounded, rational knowledge. The parallel for university instruction is how a student can become expert when his educational experiences are repetitive and reproductive, how a preparatory phase in which materials are memorized and absorbed can be transformed into critical conviction. The question is nothing less than how a person can, on the basis of his prior experiences, become a responsible, rational, and knowledgeable human being. I have noted the many ways in which contemporary university fails to confront the paradox of learning directly, though it acknowledges it implicitly by thoroughly separating preparatory from consummatory phases of understanding, so that the development of insight is effectively left to the student, to be achieved in what are effectively miraculous and uncontrolled ways.

The major step required for the resolution of the paradox is the abolition of the sharp distinction between knowledge and ignorance. This dissolution must occur from both sides. There are effective cognitive powers in the child which provide the basis for his cognitive development; at the advanced stages of research and discovery, the same general powers are employed, enriched by use but still fallible and incomplete. Learning is discovery, at every level of development, and the methods employed in discovery are given by query. Yet many strains of contemporary thought have attempted to dissolve the paradox from one side only. Following Kant, the main stream of epistemological theories which would explain how knowledge can be acquired emphasize what they take to be the structures and organizing principles which underlie all phases of human activity, even in the young child. In their view, knowledge does not emerge from ignorance, as if the precognitive organism were a mechanical system, but is a development from innate organizing and cognizing systems. We may include here philosophers and psychologists ranging from Kant to Hegel, Chomsky to Piaget. All take the position that without antecedently established cognitive conditions, the development of advanced knowledge and insight would be impossible. They differ as to the particular structures and conditions which must be presupposed, and whether they are essentially static and unchanging or themselves developed through the development of the individual and society.

I have contrasted such theories of precognitive cognition with a more flexible emphasis on the powers of the mind grounded in the *Meno* in a theory of inquiry and generalized to a theory of insight and query. Such a theory relaxes the assumptions generating the paradox of learning from both sides. It accepts the principle that no understanding can emerge from a state prior to knowledge that is entirely non-cognitive: understanding and insight must be presupposed at all phases of organic activity, even in the infant, powers of organizing experience in reliable and effective ways. However, such powers may not be grounded in specific cognitive systems, but are effectively the powers of inference, hypothesis, judgment, theory-construction, and generalization that make query possible. Following Socrates, we must take for granted the powers of the mind that are necessary to query. They may be strengthened or refined, but they are present as part of the organic system of human responses, at least in incipient form. From the other side, we may define knowledge as the outcome of successful query—where success is grounded in query itself and its developing standards. There is no state of the normal human being that is entirely *pre*cognitive; there is no state of the cognizing adult that is the possession of knowledge free from admixture with ignorance, incompleteness, and error. The consequences for science and philosophy are that knowledge is in a profound sense always limited, fallible, and inexhaustible; the consequences for elementary and university instruction are that preparatory, "precognitive", phases of instruction must be avoided, and query, invention, and discovery emphasized at every stage.

The general principle that embodies this approach to the development of understanding is that *learning is discovery*. I will delineate a theory of instruction based on this principle and explore some of its implications for the political and intellectual obligations of the university. The more general principle may be interpreted in terms of a number of other, subsidiary principles that underlie the theory of insight. Several of these have been mentioned in the course of earlier discussions.[1]

1) *Invention.* The principle is formulated most effectively by Piaget: *to understand is to invent.* But it is found in a great many other theories of cognitive development and understanding. In its strongest form—and I have argued that only in this form does it provide a resolution of the paradox of learning—it defines not a *desirable* condition of understanding, but a *necessary condition,* a *criterion* of understanding. As Chomsky, argues, linguistic competence is not intelligible as the repetition of strings of words, but as the production and understanding of novel sentences and combinations of sentences (see page 5).

Chomsky appears to hold that novelty in linguistic utterance requires an explanation, found in a universal grammar based on innate linguistic principles. Yet the point is much stronger if we ask what linguistic competence might mean if it did not include novelty and invention. As a form of knowledge, competence is always an ability to understand and to produce new linguistic products. Piaget also suggests that invention is something to be explained, although he recognizes that it is a defining condition of understanding (see passage on p. 5). If to understand is to invent, invention must be presupposed as a power of the mind, grounded in insight and in query.

I am proposing that the principle of invention be taken as a criterion of understanding, which leads directly to a theory of insight. Mere reproduction is not understanding. To learn a language is to become able to utter and understand sentences never encountered before; to learn mathematics is to become able to solve new problems in new ways and to apply information in novel contexts. Piaget and Chomsky are correct in believing that something stronger than a reproductive theory of cognitive development is required to explain such invention. However, their claim that innate structures and organizing systems must be postulated for such explanation is controversial and, in many ways, too confining. The point is that invention is a pervasive characteristic of all understanding, and is grounded in the pervasiveness of insight as one of the fundamental powers of the mind. We may seek to explain *how* invention is possible, but not in ways that would confine inventive powers beyond the requirements of insight and query.

2) *Transcendence.*   The principle of invention lends itself to reformulation and generalization in the principle that *learning always transcends the available materials*.[2] This is the principle of transcendence, and is to be understood in the same criteriological terms as the principle of invention. Not only do we hope that students will go beyond the materials presented to them, not only do we observe that they sometimes do so, but such transcendence to novel situations and applications is a criterion of understanding. All theories of cognitive development presuppose transcendence at least to the extent that generalization and organization are involved. Even a reproductive, combinatorial model of the mind presupposes transcendence in the novel combinations generated by mental processes.[3] The question is whether new

insights, theories, and modes of understanding are to be taken for granted where understanding is possessed.

I have noted the educational implications of the principle of transcendence and the implicit acquiescence of university teachers in the paradox of learning: that *knowledge can be learned but cannot be taught*. Learning here refers to the transcendent and novel insights attained by a student to the extent that he goes beyond what is presented to him. Virtually by definition, if understanding means transcendence, what is learned cannot be taught to the extent that it involves going beyond the presented materials. The preparatory phase of instruction is then simply the presentation of materials to the student. Some students, it is assumed, will come to understanding in their own terms, essentially on their own, through the powers of their minds. The principle that learning is discovery accepts the latter assumption, but it also assumes that it is the responsibility of the teacher to encourage the development of insight and the achievement of discoveries.

3) *Implicit Knowledge.* It is clear from the systematic and organizational character of knowledge and query that in order to know one thing, we must know many other things. A stronger, and more important position, however, is the innatist Kantian position which says that in order to understand certain forms of knowledge — such as linguistic competence — we must look to implicit, underlying forms of knowledge that a person may employ and even discover, but which he does not need to be able to formulate in order to use. The principle involved here is that *all explicit forms of understanding are based on an implicit knowledge that can be formulated and expressed only to a limited extent.* In its strongest form, the principle suggests that knowledge is grounded on genetically determined cognitive principles and attitudes. Linguistic competence in Chomsky is based on a universal and innate grammatical disposition. Even in a developmental theory like Piaget's, the impetus to cognitive development rests on a cognitive system present even in the newborn infant. Closely related to the principle of implicit knowledge is the principle of structure: that *meaning implies*

structure.[4] In a loose sense, entailing that meaning and understanding always presuppose organizational and theoretical principles, the principle of structure is plausible but ineffective. In the stronger sense, suggesting that a uniform organizational system is present throughout all human development and understanding, the principle is highly implausible, though with some important and specific applications.

The innatist and structuralist positions are the stronger versions of the principle of implicit knowledge. They explain invention by appeal to a stable basis of transcendent principles. The irony here is that invention is explained by a static and unchanging cognitive system. Piaget's genetic theory is only a bit better in this respect, since it rests on an unvarying sequence of cognitive stages. What is wrong with most of these neo-Kantian and neo-Hegelian theories is that they postulate a uniform and stable system of implicit knowledge to explain the immense variation in cognitive systems among human beings and throughout human history.

The theory of insight and query I have been advocating, after Socrates' suggestions in the *Meno,* assumes only a capacity to improve the cognitive powers of the mind. Invention and transcendence are characteristic traits of insight, and the indeterminate, immediate qualities of insight define what is implicit in every explicit understanding. The theory of insight rests on the principle that there is understanding only where there is insight — *no insight, no understanding.* It includes the principles of invention, transcendence, and implicit knowledge without controversial and implausible commitments to particular, innate, underlying structural principles that cannot be modified with experience.

Something of course is innate: all theories agree on that. They differ on whether what is innate is more mechanical than cognitive, causal rather than rule-based, static rather than changeable. Mechanical reproductive theories, where invention is at best combinatorial, run directly afoul of the paradox of learning. They require knowledge to be derived from non-cognitive elements and conditions. Transcendence and invention are minimized, and the development of new theories and viewpoints is especially unintelligible. Most important, they reject the principle of implicit knowledge and with it the principle of insight. All knowledge can be traced in principle to the elements that comprise it and their combinations. Neo-Kantian theories like Chomsky's and the structuralists' postulate unvarying organizing principles that conform to the principles of invention, transcendence, and implicit knowledge, but with fundamental limitations grounded in the universality and innateness of the principles which are the basis of cognition. Neo-Hegelian theories like Piaget's allow for the development of new kinds of theories and the development of new modes of cognition, but in an unvarying and preprogrammed sequence. All these theories are highly restrictive of the powers of the mind, though they presume to explain the strongest of such powers.

Only theories of insight and query can fully accommodate the power of the principles of invention, transcendence, and implicit knowledge without overly rigid commitments to the forms knowledge may take. It may be worth noting here two subsidiary hypotheses that are compatible with insight theories and which can bridge the gap between prior experience and the development of novel modes of cognition. One can be found in John Dewey's work and also in some recent studies of language development: that children develop language by a process of overgeneralization. They extend theories, concepts, and rules far more widely than would be appropriate on the basis of an inductive model, and learn to restrict the boundaries of generalization through counter-instances.[5] It is clear that this is an epistemic principle: hypotheses are generated relative to the applicability of concepts and rules which are defined on the basis of evidence. Every rule, concept, or cognitive element is epistemic and theoretical in this sense, generating novel hypotheses which are restricted through subsequent experience to plausible and justifiable domains of application. Transcendence here is the fundamental principle, with invention following as a matter of course, while the generalizing tendency provides a form of insight based on a powerful range of cognitive hypotheses that cannot be fully explicated.

Closely related to this hypothesis is a principle of "leaping to conclusions": "The associative memory by its nature goes from recognition of particular items, each possessing some common characteristic, to the recognition of the characteristic itself."[6] Cooper and Moskowitz are proposing much weaker hypotheses of innate conditions to generate theory construction and sophisticated knowledge (of language and science) than we find in Chomsky and Piaget. The important thing to note about Cooper's hypothesis is that the *leap* of generalization is essentially what I have regarded as insight. He seems to treat it as a mechanical, routine activity of the mind. To the extent that it is not divisible into smaller steps — though it is intelligible and understandable in an indefinite number of other ways — it is a characteristic of the mind that we can employ but not mediate. It is in this sense (and only in this sense) immediate, one of the primary characteristics of insight. An additional point to emphasize is that the leap is to a *conclusion,* and is in this sense epistemic and cognitive. The mind here is fundamentally cognitive, constructing hypotheses and theories on the basis of past experience, and doing so directly and effectively. Of course, none of these theories may conform to the nature of things; they require a match between the powers of the mind and the order of nature. Kant emphasizes this point in his *Third Critique,* but he postulates too strong a character to the mind. Where theories are closer to experience, constantly undergoing modification on the basis of such experience, a far weaker assumption of natural order is required.

There is a natural tension inherent in the principles of transcendence and implicit knowledge that in many writings approaches scepticism. On the one hand, knowledge cannot emerge from entirely noncognitive conditions, so we must postulate cognitive conditions inherent in the mind. These establish the possibility of knowledge, but they may also be viewed as limitations upon our ability to respond to natural conditions directly. The principle of transcendence defines the ability of the mind to go beyond what is presented to it as a necessary condition, a criterion, of understanding. But the supplementation that is inherent in transcendence may also be viewed from a sceptical point of view, as marking a deviation from the datum.

A useful example is T.S. Kuhn's well-known account in

Structure of Scientific Revolutions. In "normal" science, research and exploration are grounded in an established paradigm of methods and theoretical presuppositions, but there are important periods of "abnormal" science where a shift of paradigm is involved, and observations and laws are given a radically different interpretation.[7]

Perhaps the best-known examples are the shift from Ptolemaic to Copernican astronomy, culminating in Newtonian theory, and the shift from Newtonian theory to relativity, neither of which can be interpreted, Kuhn argues, as simply grounded in new evidence. There is a close analogue here to inventive insights within an overarching sphere of understanding and inventive insights which transform the way we understand a particular cognitive domain: non-constitutive and constitutive insights. Both forms of cognitive development are extremely important.

The Kuhnian account is controversial, and has been criticized from both sides. On the one hand, it appears to offer no grounds other than social practice for a shift in paradigm. The incommensurability of paradigms suggests that no entirely rational grounds can determine a choice among them. On the other hand, Kuhn has been criticized for overemphasizing the revolutionary character of a paradigm shift, since the success of a scientific theory, it is argued, is a function of complex social strategies, never evidential grounds alone.[8] On the one hand, the development of science transcends the available evidence in paradigms which are not justified by the evidence, but effectively define what will be accepted as evidence. On the other hand, science is but a strategy for producing social consensus, however that is produced. Both views can be given a sceptical interpretation.

Several important principles are suggested by Kuhn's account which are somewhat less controversial than his revolutionary theory, and which are essential to the theory of insight: 1) observations and facts are known and understood only when located in a relational context given by a more comprehensive vision or theory; 2) a plurality of diverse insights are relevant to any given subject matter, and these are related by overlapping and similarity, by method and submethod, insight and sub-insight, but there is no overarching synthesis of all visions in a comprehensive understanding; 3) the source of novel insights is often unknown, since it involves a synthesis of other insights which can be only partially explicated, yet the only way we have of controlling novel insights is through query—which is simultaneously process and outcome in cognitive development and discovery; 4) query is the source of major insights as well as the only means we have of evaluating insights. Ultimately, then, it is the interrogative and unlimited character of query that is the solution to the paradox of learning.

The Kuhnian account of scientific development and the principles just enunciated have frequently been viewed in a sceptical light. Analogously, Wittgenstein's grounding of knowledge in the fabric of social life suggests to many that no criteria other than social practice can be a basis of knowledge. Similarly, Derrida's claim that there is writing and only writing—including science as writing—suggests that there is a fundamental arbitrariness inherent in all scientific conclusions, for they are grounded in the linguistic and social conditions of scientific practice.[9]

All of these views follow, in one form or another, the first three principles above, but they neglect the force of principle (4): the nature of query. They effectively resolve the paradox of learning by dissipating the distinction between ignorance and belief from the side of knowledge, leaving us with a sceptical view toward knowledge. They regard the source of knowledge in query as a limitation rather than an achievement, a tension inherent in human cognitive powers. What is at stake is precisely the powers which we must assume we possess if knowledge is possible—and if learning is possible as well. We confront the paradox of learning again. The resolution of the paradox requires us to weaken the distinction between knowledge and ignorance from both sides: not only from the side of knowledge, but relative to the achievements of query. Query is the origin of knowledge as well as its criterion.

The rejection of absolute and systematic grounds for knowledge appears to lead to scepticism. Yet it can lead there only through query. We cannot be sceptical of query if we must employ query to ground our scepticism. There are no epistemic grounds outside query, for query is the process whereby information is collected and insight is developed to produce under-standing and validation. What is presupposed is that query includes whatever self-critical and rational methods we can develop to make truth and falsity intelligible.

This point was understood by Charles Sanders Peirce in his definition of truth in relation to scientific query: "the opinion which is fated to be ultimately agreed to by all who investigate, is what we mean by the truth".[10] The definition is obviously inadequate unless we include Peirce's insight that the method of science is the only effective means for criticizing its own shortcomings. The methods of query are self-critical in the sense that they include all means of rational evaluation and correction.

We have here one of the striking reasons for extending the scope of query beyond that of inquiry: if inquiry is the method of scientific query, then science needs more than itself for self-criticism and self-correction. This is particularly true in the social and behavioral sciences, where philosophical, normative, and sociological issues have been shown to be relevant to the most empirical considerations. It is true even in the physical sciences insofar as they involve methodological assumptions requiring logical criticism and systematic assumptions that effectively encroach on other fields of query.

The conclusion is that the resolution of the paradox of learning, if it is to be epistemologically effective, must weaken the gap between knowledge and ignorance from both sides, thereby strengthening the achievements of query. As Socrates suggests, we must have faith in our powers of inquiry—for otherwise we could reach no conclusions, sceptical or otherwise. We cannot be sceptical about query, not systematically and in principle, for we would then have no intelligible means for either defending or criticizing our scepticism. We may criticize any achievement, any conclusion, of query, of insight, any claim, any judgment; such criticism is part of query itself. But we cannot reject query, insight, understanding altogether. Likewise, though all under-standing requires invention and transcendence, these cannot possibly be the basis of a sceptical position. Rather, we must recognize that transcendence is the source of knowledge and discovery, not its impediment, and leads to the continuing and unending, interrogative and self-critical activities which comprise query.

The sceptical position is systematically incoherent, and cannot be followed consistently. Nevertheless, there are two important insights expressed by it. First, it emphasizes the dissolution of the gap between ignorance and knowledge from the side of knowledge, emphasizing the incompleteness of all understanding and the relevance of further query. It errs in failing to emphasize the dissolution from the side of ignorance, so that cognitive powers are taken for granted in the activities of query. Second, it emphasizes the indeterminateness in all epistemological determinations (and in all other determinations as well: the complementary relationship of determinateness and indeterminateness in knowledge and being).[11] This is the fundamental source of unending query. Nevertheless, the point again is that not only is indeterminateness relative to all determinateness, but conversely, there is determinateness in all indeterminateness: the basis ultimately of knowledge and query as well as of being and identity. Knowledge is possible because everything is determinate in many ways, and we are capable of understanding it; the acquisition of knowledge is possible, however, because everything is indeterminate in many ways, calling for continuing and unending query. The tension inherent in the limits of understanding is mirrored in the conjoint effectiveness and interminability of query, which reflects the conjoint interrelationship of determinateness and indeterminateness in the nature of things.

An additional principle of understanding beyond those of invention, transcendence, and implicit knowledge is required and embodied within the theory of insight, though it is not obviously included within the other theories considered above. I call this the principle of *assimilation: a person understands something only when it belongs to him, when he can take credit for knowing it.*[12] The paradox of learning, as I have construed it, raises the question of how the testimony of others can be transformed into knowledge possessed by an agent. On a reproductive model, experiences and testimony remain *external,* only repeated and recombined in the mind. Without assuming an innate capacity of understanding or insight, it is impossible to explain how such elements can comprise knowledge. Neo-Kantian and Neo-Hegelian theories assimilate experiences and testimony to innate principles of the mind, becoming known because of the ways in which they are assimilated. However, the assumptions are too strong, since even the innate programming is in a sense external to the agent—a consequence of evolutionary development, for example. His theories are not what he knows, personally, but how he responds on the basis of genetic programming.

The principle of invention offers a solution to this difficulty. A man understands something as a responsible agent only when he understands it and its justification *uniquely*. What he shares with everyone else may be either duplicated and reproduced or a consequence of mechanical responses. Invention is the essential criterion of understanding, and a criterion as well of transcendence, implicit knowledge, and assimilation. The invention that establishes personal assimilation, however, is not a universal competence, but a personal range of applications and insights. However public and universal certain truths may be—as they are in science—they are known and assimilated by the agent only relative to his personal, often idiosyncratic, insights into novel implications and applications. The idiosyncrasy should not be overemphasized: there are many forms of knowledge which, in all public manifestations, we share in common with others. Yet these public forms, I am arguing, rest on insights that are not uniform among all knowers, but rest on personal and varying insights and sub-insights. These may often be subtle and covert, modest variations of standard norms. Implicit knowledge is frequently variable with insight and experience. It should be noted how the hypotheses of overgeneralization and leaping to conclusions are compatible with such an emphasis on personal knowledge. The experiences that generate the peripheries of constricted overgeneralizations are unique for every individual, and vary with every individual. This may be a continuing source of novel hypotheses necessary to the advancement of knowledge (as well as of aberrant hypotheses which prove useless and indefensible).

This entire discussion confirms the fundamental principle that learning is discovery. It is discovery because it always involves invention, novel insights, and understandings, and because it is assimilated to the personal experiences and insights of the agent. However, learning is grounded in implicit forms of knowledge that go beyond the data presented, and in this sense is discovery in the context of epistemic, cognitive hypotheses and conceptions. The paradox of learning is eliminated by the principle that learning is discovery in the nature of insight as a novel, personal, inventive transformation of one mode of insight into another.

Learning and understanding, then, are grounded in insight. I have noted the fundamental properties of insight: immediacy, relationality, and fallibility. Insight here is a theory- or hypothesis-generating power, a power of *judgment,* not a truth-giving power. It comes with no guarantees and there is no way of providing such guarantees from within. Were there such, knowledge would be produced by them, not through query. The paradox of learning would be unresolvable. Insight is not only fallible, but is often wrong, in whole or in part. Just as many conclusions reached must be modified — even rejected — on the basis of counter-evidence, many insights must be rejected, transformed by other insights, on the basis of evidence. Nevertheless, erroneous insights play an important role in the development of new and more effective insights: the truth and the fruitfulness of insights are frequently only tenuously related.

Insight is modifiable only by other insights; it is in that sense irreplaceable in understanding. In the same sense, insight is immediate in that it is a leap from data to conclusion that can be grounded only in insight. Of course, just as it is fallible, insight is modifiable. It can be trained, developed, strengthened, improved. In all cases, however, understanding of such improvement is realized only through other insights. Another way of putting this is to state that understanding always depends on hypotheses generated from present data by a mind trained through its past experiences — and these hypotheses always go beyond the data in a direct, novel, and unmediated fashion. Insights are immediate in the sense that nothing can mediate them except other insights.

The relational character of insight is the basis of its cognitive qualities, generating hypotheses and theories, principles and rules. There are insights into differences as well as similarities, into uniqueness as well as resemblance. But all such insights are relational, not in the bald sense in which difference is a relation, but in the sense in which differences depend on organizing perspectives for their intelligibility. Difference and similarity are always *in a certain respect,* relevant *in certain ways.* Insight into differences is intelligible only when grounded in a larger insight into the respects in which these differences are relevant.

All understanding depends on insight; all learning is the development of insight. The fundamental question of education, then, is how novel and important insights are to be attained. This is the same question as that of the advancement of knowledge. Learning is discovery in the sense that both the advance of human knowledge and the development of individual understanding are fundamentally the same. I will not presume here to prescribe specific techniques for the improvement of insight in either the student or the expert. I will simply examine the consequences for instruction and for university participants of an educational theory founded on insight rather than preparation and repetition.

CHAPTER 9

Discovery

There are two ways of looking at the discoveries possible within cognitive activities. There is discovery that adds to human knowledge. There is also discovery brought by query relative to its prior conditions. This is discovery for the learner upon application of a cognitive method, in some cases, discovery of a new cognitive method. Except for transcendent discoveries which transform human knowledge and the methods of acquiring it, both kinds of discovery are alike relative to the methods employed. Both rely on established cognitive powers and on insight and invention. They are indistinguishable relative to the learner's activities and powers. They are distinguishable only in relation to the history of mankind. This is the basis of the principle that learning is discovery.

The entire discussion up to this point has laid the basis for this conclusion. Knowledge is produced by query: learning is then the result of query, based on insight and invention. Even learning by memorization and repetition can become knowledge only through the insight and understanding that is the result of query. The difference between novice and expert does not lie in the presence of insight and invention, in the application of query in the one case and not the other, but in the conditions of the queries they each undertake, the complexity of the insights they possess, the norms on which their inventions are based and against which they are tested. Even the youngest infant possesses rudimentary cognitive skills that comprise elementary forms of query. Without them, we would never be able to acquire the more sophisticated skills that constitute the most advanced systems of thought and understanding.

Insight and query are the basis of learning, but some people are better at certain forms of query than others, some activities of query are more productive than others. Nevertheless, the fact that learning does take place, that discoveries are made, is testimony to a general human capacity to develop and improve cognitive powers through insight and query, to become more effective in cognitive undertakings. How this capacity is to be maximized is the question of prime concern at both instructional and advanced phases of cognitive development.

The fundamental principle of the theory of discovery is that learning for the student is not qualitatively different from the discoveries of the expert, based on a preparatory model of instruction. Rather, the expert's discoveries establish the paradigm for all cognitive development, the development of the mind by the activities of query. An equally fundamental principle of the theory, however, is that there are many different kinds of query, many different methods and submethods, each of which is related to many others, but which are not all interrelated or reducible to some supreme method or form of query. The difference between expert and novice is far more like the difference between persons who engage in different kinds of query, which can be related by further query, than between a person who is a master of a branch of query and another who is ignorant of it. The fundamental problem of cognitive development is always how to move from one kind or level of query to another, with query our only means of development. Query is the only link we have among the insights required in different branches and at different levels of understanding.

The conclusion is that learning and discovery are fundamentally the same for master and student. Both forms of learning are the result of query: a methodic activity in which discoveries are made. They differ in specific applications and conclusions, but not in the importance of insight, invention, discovery, transcendence, and assimilation. The most important and immediate application of this conclusion is the rejection of a theoretical distinction between preparatory and consummatory stages of learning. We cannot mortgage the present to the future where powers of the mind are concerned, for they are both means and end together. The powers that we seek to encourage — of insight, invention, and discovery — must be developed through insight, invention, and discovery, not held in abeyance through years of preparation. Preparation without discovery is not learning but repetition. Discovery without preparation is unintelligible. The two are unified in the activity of query, which is both result and means simultaneously.

The pedagogical principle which is entailed by this view of learning is one of familiarity: *learning as discovery is made upon familiar materials,* while *query is the methodic means to familiarity.* We may consider once again the method described by David Hawkins in teaching science to children. I must quote at length.

there is a time, much greater in amount than commonly allowed, which should be devoted to free and unguided exploratory work (call it play if you wish; I call it work). Children are given materials and equipment — *things* — and are allowed to construct, test, probe, and experiment without superimposed questions or instruction. I call this phase "Messing About".... In starting this way I, for one, naively assumed that a couple of hours of "Messing About" would suffice. After two hours, instead, we allowed two more and, in the end, a stretch of several weeks. In all this time, there was little or no evidence of boredom or confusion. Most of the questions we might have planned for came up unscheduled.

Why did we permit this length of time? First, because in our previous classes we had noticed that things went well when we veered toward "Messing About" and not as well when we held too tight a rein on what we wanted the children to do. It was clear that these children had had insufficient acquaintance with the sheer phenomena of pendulum motion and needed to build an apperceptive background, against which a more analytical sort of knowledge could take form and make sense.... Second, we allowed things to develop this way because we decided we were getting a new kind of feedback from the children and were eager to see where and by what paths their interests would evolve and carry them. We were rewarded with a higher level of involvement and a much greater diversity of experiments.... There were many sorts of discoveries made, but we let them slip by without much adult resonance, beyond our spontaneous and manifest enjoyment of the phenomena. So discoveries were made, noted, lost, and made again. I think this is why the slightly pontifical phrase "discovery method" bothers me. When learning is at the most fundamental level, as it is here, with all the abstractions of Newtonian mechanics just around the corner, don't rush! When the mind is evolving the abstractions which will lead to physical comprehension, all of us must cross the line between ignorance and insight many times before we truly understand....

This ("Messing About") phase is important, above all, because it carries over into school that which is the source of most of what children have already learned, the roots of their moral, intellectual, and esthetic enjoyment. If education were defined, for the moment, to include everything that has come to them from living in the natural and human world, then by any sensible measure what has come before age five or six would outweigh all the rest. When we narrow the scope of education to what goes on in schools, we throw out the method of that early and spectacular progress at our peril....

If you once let children evolve their own learning along paths of their own choosing, you then must see it through and *maintain* the individuality of their work. You cannot begin that way and then say, in effect, "That was only a teaser", thus using your adult authority to devalue what the children themselves, in the meantime, have found most valuable.[13]

Three principles may be singled out:

1) If a person is given enough time and material, in a situation he must largely structure for himself, he will invent things to do and will make many discoveries.

2) A person must be given time to become very familiar with the materials from which he is to fashion his discoveries.[14]

3) When the mind is developing the insights that comprise understanding, all of us must cross the line between ignorance and insight many times before we truly understand.

I will consider these principles in reverse order.

All of us must cross the line between ignorance and insight many times before we truly understand. This is the fundamental principle upon which a solution to the paradox of learning rests, for it undercuts the sharpness of the distinction between ignorance and knowledge, indicates the central role of insight, and emphasizes the tentative, fallible, and processive nature of query. Properly speaking, of course, "true understanding" is but more of the same: insight and query involving continual interrogation and discovery. The most important features of Hawkins' principle, however, are its implications for instruction. Learning is a matter of crossing and re-crossing from ignorance to understanding, a matter of insights alternating with confusion and then new insights, a continual mixture of insight, understanding, and confusion.

Students frequently complain that their "understanding" is not adequately tested in examinations, only their ability to translate what they know into words or performance. The natural reply, that they do not understand what they cannot say, is only partly true. The fuller truth is that these students only partly know, not only because they are students, but because knowledge can never be complete. They understand some aspects of what they have studied, some applications in some perspectives. The examination presents them with a particular context in which to make application and to display understanding, while they may possess considerable insight relative to other contexts and applications. The examination system effectively assumes that a single test of understanding can be made, as if there were a sharp line between knowledge and ignorance, a single, universal criterion of understanding.

There is a profound disparity between the preparatory and examination procedures found in many university classes and the substance of Hawkins' principle. The disparity is expressed most forcefully in the common if implicit belief of those who teach in a university that no course alone provides understanding of a field, nor can a student be expected to know everything taught in a course. Even the best students will forget certain details and will fail to understand some of the ramifications of important principles. A student is never expected to learn more than a part of a university course, yet he is expected to have that part ready on call on a particular date and in a predetermined form.

The importance of insight in learning entails that understanding is always partial at a given time. Moreover, there is an alternation of confusion and insight, varying over time and in different respects. There is no moment when a principle has been fully understood in all its significance, for important principles have an indefinite number of complex ramifications, and may be viewed in an indefinite number of different ways. In some contexts, a partial insight is tantamount to *no* insight. For this reason, a system of education based on learning in a specific time and place, measured by performance on uniform examinations, tends to emphasize facts which can be memorized and counted. The question of understanding is simply postponed; repetition is accepted as a substitute for insight.

The conclusion is not that examinations must encourage students rather than penalize them, must reward success rather than punish failure. Hawkins' principle entails that we should reappraise the entire system of instruction in relation to the passage of time. Understanding cannot be divided into pieces, each to be ingested on a particular day. Particular insights come and go. The credit system of education, devised to pass as large a number of students as possible through the university, requires the production of degrees, courses, and answers on examinations *all on time.* Learning, which proceeds in fits and starts, has become as regimented as a factory. The result has been a sense of oppression, a fear of failure, and the establishment of mediocre expectations. If students are all to be run through a maze together, in a fixed time, then we may expect only an average performance from them in that time. There is no systematic provision for judging whether some or many students have come to a deeper understanding in their own time. Time is very important in life, but it is effectively extrinsic to discovery and learning. These exercise their own constraints and impose their own shape on time and activity.

The time required for discovery brings us to our second principle: *A person must have time to become very familiar with the materials from which he will fashion his discoveries.* This is a principle of play. Learning as discovery comes with a play with an of ideas and things. For it is only through familiarity gained by such play that a person comes to an understanding for himself. We can learn what others make us learn to satisfy them — facts and answers. But we understand only when we think for ourselves and by ourselves. Play, familiarity, and understanding take time — the student's time, however, not the teacher's.

The growth of a child of the universe into an autonomous, individual member of a culture takes place essentially in the realm of play. For the essence of play is that it is an apparently *unnecessary* activity ... appropriate for later use in the conscious and deliberate pursuit of serious ends.[15]

This principle is not merely neglected in university education, it is actively opposed. A beginning student in a laboratory science is given twenty-five unfamiliar problems to solve each week and is required to perform preassigned tasks in his laboratory with unfamiliar equipment. He has no time to play, either with the problems or the equipment. Nor does he want to. We may imagine what would happen if students were given free run in a laboratory, to devise and complete a project of their own, under supervision and with help. How many more would make discoveries significant at least to themselves? In beginning language courses, the textbook defines what will be learned, class by class and week by week. Yet everyone knows of the relative success of saturation courses in foreign languages. May this success not be due to the opportunity a student has to play with the language as he employs it — to pun in it, laugh at his errors, grope in it, *familiarize* himself with it: to learn of it in his own good time, though not necessarily a very long time?

Does the principle of familiarity entail that learning must always begin with the student's prior understanding, as Hawkins suggests? Unquestionably. Does it entail that education must be "relevant" or "practical"? Only for students who are familiar only with practical things. Does it entail that learning will be restricted by the student's prior interests, that students will learn less than they do at present? This is the critical question. Hawkins' point, which I am supporting, is that students will learn *more,* and move *faster* (though in fits and starts), if they are given enough time to become familiar with their materials, enough time to develop the essential relevant insights. They will learn to think for themselves; they will develop their own insights. This is the burden of Hawkins' first principle, that *if a person is given enough time and material, in a situation he must largely structure for himself, he will invent things to do and will make many discoveries.*[16] We commonly assume that students will learn to think for themselves, and gain novel insights, *after* instruction is over. Hawkins' principle asks us to incorporate such expectations directly into the instructional process.

How, it may be asked, is a student to become familiar with the complexities of economic theory, the details of a historical period, the grammar of an unknown language, or the thought of Spinoza? That is indeed the question for university education. Let me suggest a modest proposal. The first two years of college will consist of a large number of readings and activities (I have laboratories in mind) with which the student is expected to become familiar. He is given the entire list of them upon admission, and he is offered — though not required to attend — a variety of courses dealing with the listed materials. At various times during the first two years he is expected to display his familiarity with some part of the materials, but he may choose among a variety of ways to do so. He may write an extended study covering several works. He may take examinations in courses he attends. He may take an examination on the details of the works on his list. He may work on individual projects. And so forth. Until he has become familiar with these materials, he cannot go on. But he is expected to gain this familiarity in his own way. Individual courses are structured along similar lines — that is, to encourage students to familiarize themselves with the course materials in their own ways. The teacher is there to provide help, to define alternatives, and to throw up his hands at ventures for which he has no respect or patience. He is also there as a shining example of the mind at work, showing by his own activities how an inventive understanding functions.

Won't students do crazy and worthless things? Some will. Nevertheless, materials provide their own constraints. There isn't much you can do with calculus but study it, work problems in it, and use it in the sciences. If a student wishes to write poetry about it, let him. He will discover that he needs to understand it first. Furthermore, our world can use a poetry based on an understanding of technology. I am not proposing that students follow their own interests exclusively, though some will do so for a time. The interests of young people are frequently impoverished and undefined. More specific interests and capabilities, however, are developed only on the basis of familiarity developed through productive and personal play. They are also to be developed in the context of the examples set by teachers and other students. Most important of all, invention and discovery, insight and understanding, are both the means and the end of all education.

Organizational and curricular changes cannot replace attention to and respect for insight; play and familiarity are to be encouraged only as they develop the mind and foster understanding as manifested by invention.

What is the role of the teacher in learning where familiarization through play is so strongly emphasized? In part, the teacher supplies an important source of materials upon which familiarity may be built. Perhaps the most important role of the teacher, however, is not as a transmitter of · insight, but as a salient example of insight and understanding — an extremely demanding role for which many teachers are not prepared, but which, at the college and university level, is the role required by the identity of learning and discovery. Students can be encouraged to think and to understand only by being present during thought and understanding, by being made aware of their own cognitive powers through witnessing the powers of others. The preparatory mode of instruction tends to obscure the development of insight in both teacher and student, presenting conclusions without the thought that entered into them. The role of the teacher, then, is as inquirer along with the student, both employing their powers of insight and discovery and developing them by use. The exemplary mode of instruction is the only mode entirely compatible with the principle of familiarity and the identity of learning and discovery.

Familiarity with many things and ideas must clearly be acquired before college. We may therefore expand the above proposal as follows: in the twelve grades through high school, students study arithmetic and the speaking and reading of several languages (including their own). Let the twelve years in other respects be relatively free play with ideas, reading, and various tools — in shop, history, laboratories, paints, philosophy, economics, languages, and mathematics. Let there be a great deal of play and little examination. Let everything a student might want to study later be included as a resource with which he may become familiar earlier. Then let those who wish go on to higher education. What will they know? How to read, speak, and think — which is everything important.

Am I not neglecting the weaker, alienated students? How will students who think that school today is a waste of their time and energy respond to so free and contentless a structure? There are many reasons why students find schools empty of significance, afflicted by incompetent and uninterested teachers, regimentation, and low expectations. I do not suppose that my suggestion will solve all the ills to which schools are prey. Rather, I am arguing that a successful school system must be founded on a positive view of human capacities, on a realistic sense of the powers of the mind. We can only help students to learn to think — in part by presenting materials to which such thought will be addressed. This is both a sublime achievement and a modest one — for we rely almost exclusively on the native powers of the students' minds. Nevertheless, the sublime powers of the mind are often obscured in preparatory phases of instruction. I am arguing that students are awakened far more by encounters with inventive minds who encourage students' inventive powers than by a regimentation and learning by rote that is thought more appropriate for undeveloped minds. I am arguing that insight is so important in learning that it should be made the center of attention rather than the facts and skills which are useless without such insight and understanding. The principle of insight resolves the importance of facts and skills in education: we can acquire facts by rote without understanding, but we cannot gain certain important insights without the relevant facts. Insight is therefore our primary concern, with all the requisite materials constitutive of it.

This entire discussion has been founded on the principle that *play is discovery*. In play there is continual exploration, learning, and discovery. A small child explores his surroundings incessantly, first by mouth, later by taking things apart and putting them together, by throwing them and breaking them. Afterward, he explores the world outside, whatever is in his environment. The child fortunate enough to grow up in the country can be and often is left to his own devices within a considerable range of territory. He plays with whatever is to be found there; he discovers what is to be discovered at a level appropriate to his development. If there is work around him, he tries to get into it. He plays as adults work, and his play is an imitation of adult work. By himself he learns how to do what they do.

This mode of play with its attendant discoveries is limited. A child on a farm may be surrounded by wildlife, yet not classify it. He may not systematically describe the varieties of birds nor the feeding habits of raccoons and beavers. The principle that play leads to discovery is mute on whether the discoveries are important. Discovery itself, along with query, is important enough and enriches itself through practice and attention. Nevertheless, there are subjects that are more important for an individual than others, in a particular social context, and there are discoveries that are more valuable for him in his particular circumstances. These are competing values, but we must not sacrifice discovery and insight to particular subject matters or skills, for they too depend on insights and discoveries.

The play of familiarity that leads to discovery is not, as Hawkins notes, to be contrasted with work, but with drudgery, repetition without insight. Discovery is the fruit of familiarity with ideas and things attained through play—a free play of imagination in which insight is predominant. In part, we are talking about variety of perspectives, a play with things that is not so much repetition as variation and transformation. We return again to query, for the play that brings familiarity is a form of query, and query depends on such a play of ideas. Query must be presupposed as a natural power of the mind; we can only refine it and encourage it.

The principle that learning is discovery, to the extent that it unifies instruction and research, entails a fourth pedagogic principle which Hawkins does not discuss, but which I have mentioned several times. He emphasizes the development of the powers of the mind, insight and discovery, through the employment of these powers. Insight is gained through insight, invention comes after a familiarity gained through play. These principles must be tempered by the principle of exemplary instruction: that *we may gain insight into the powers of the mind in only two ways—by employing those powers ourselves, in the development of our own insights and by witnessing a mind in action.* Instruction, then, has two major strands: exemplification and exhortation—learning by encounter with an active, inventive mind, and learning by the development of insight through personal invention. Transcendental theories of cognitive development tend to emphasize the characteristics of the mind which make invention and understanding possible. They therefore minimize social interactions, and make the role of teachers and parents inexplicable and unimportant. The most important role teachers may play, I am suggesting, is exemplary: displaying the mind in action, encouraging the development of insight by showing how insight can be developed and employed. Such exemplification can be exhibited in many different contexts, in books and lectures as well as discussions and investigations. The goal is the development of students' minds through query. The means is always the same: query itself. Instruction by example is nothing but the pursuit of query, carried on by students and teachers together; nothing but the continuing pursuit of knowledge in collective and individual terms.

We may summarize this discussion for university education. The goal of education is the achievement of understanding—a sense of the interconnections and systematic unity of a subject, insight into its significant relations and forms. Learning is discovery, achieved through insight and query. In the same sense, a scholar learns through query as he discovers new interpretations and new evidence to support them. In this respect, a university is not divided between teaching and research, but is a collective enterprise of discovery, of the development and transmission of insight and understanding through query, taking place in a great variety of ways. Learning is not memorization by rote, not the mere repetition of assigned tasks until repeatable without thought. It is not mindless, but requires understanding. Far too often, however, learning is presented as a never-ending preparation for later insights. Most schooling is sheer preparation, unending practice and drill in textbooks which offer no grounds or explanation, the memorization of materials needed for later life. Understanding is continually postponed until suddenly, when school is over, the student discovers he was supposed to have understood before. In many cases it has become too late.

The play I have described as the source of discovery is not recreation, but creation. It is not the play of games but the play of a dramatist — the play of characters, ideas, themes, and words. To play is to revel in one's abilities with no motive but that of mastery and exploration. Of course, in human life it is seldom possible nor desirable that aims and goals be abandoned. I am therefore speaking of play within the context of important life goals. Time is taken for invention and construction, for exploration and study. We take a few minutes longer for an appointment and explore the neighborhood. We allow extra time in cooking to try new recipes, even to invent some. We take somewhat longer in reading a book to compare it with similar works we have read elsewhere, or check out some of its claims. Reading is often a kind of play in which ulterior motives are subordinated to insight and learning.

The dialectical method, exemplified in the Platonic dialogues, is a paradigm of play. What is wrong with the dialogue between Socrates and Meno's slave is precisely the drab and weary exchange of leading questions and answers. The rest of the dialogue glitters with hidden issues, with humor and obscure intimations. Even the *Republic,* though largely in the prosaic form of leading questions and affirmative answers, is replete with ironies and procrastinations. The dialectical method is the perpetual play of ideas. Through it no claim can remain untested. Through it all connections are scrutinized and reformulated. Through it a person learns a truth *for* himself *as* a truth, for he learns it by examining it and applying it in a great variety of contexts, from an unrestricted range of points of view.

Discovery is participation, not a spectator sport. A student who reads without thought, watches a film, casually writes a paper, is not learning and discovering. It is sometimes said that learning is hard work. This is false if it entails a sense of onerous labor. It is true if what is meant is that learning is dedicated play. A would-be chess player works or plays long hours. So also, a student must strain himself and his ideas, must extend his grasp of things. Many university students have the mistaken impression that study is labor, and desire that it occupy only a proportional part of their time — thirty-five to forty hours per week. They have been misled by the preparatory and disciplinary model of instruction. Learning is the development of the mind, the release of capacities by their employment. It can have no intrinsic limits of time or effort, for it is the expression of what makes us human. I include here, of course, all the cognitive powers of the mind, including social, personal, emotional, affective, skillful, athletic, as well as intellectual powers.

What of the *serious* side of university education? What of grades and certification? These are not incompatible with learning as play and discovery, though in some cases we may wish to postpone certification to the final stages of instruction. What is important is that where grades are given for memorization by rote, then students learn by rote. They may even learn *not* to discover, *not* to understand, *not* to venture on their own. If they can get high grades by not venturing down new pathways, they will not venture. It is not grades as such that are miseducational, but grades which oppose the development of insight and under- standing. We are concerned with developing the powers of the mind — powers that involve invention, discovery, insight, and query. In the end, the means we must employ are the means of query, encouraging students through query to learn to reason, to understand, to think, and to explain. Such activities can be evaluated. More important, they represent the powers that scholars, researchers, and professionals need themselves. We must abolish the myth of preparation, and replace it with instructional activities that encourage insight and discovery at every phase. These are the only cognitive powers worth striving for.

REFERENCES

1. For a detailed discussion of these principles, see my "Invention, Understanding, and the University", *Educational Theory,* Summer 1979, pp. 211-227.
2. See Jerome Bruner: *Beyond the Information Given,* J. M. Anglin (ed.), New York, Norton, 1974.
3. See Henri Poincaré: "Mathematical Creation", reprinted in Brewster Ghiselin: *The Creative Process,* Berkeley, University of California Press, 1952.

4. Philip Pettit: *The Concept of Structuralism,* Berkeley and Los Angeles, University of California Press, 1977.
5. John Dewey: *Experience and Nature,* La Salle, Illinois, Open Court, 2nd ed., 1929, p. 188; Breyne Arlene Moskowitz: "The Acquisition of Language", *Scientific American,* November 1978.
6. Leon N. Cooper: "Source and Limits of Human Intellect", *Daedalus,* Spring 1980, 109; 2, p. 9.
7. Kuhn, *The Structure of Scientific Revolutions*; see also my *The Scientific Process,* The Hague, Martinus Nijhoff, 1971.
8. Feyerabend, *Against Method.*
9. Wittgenstein, *Philosophical Investigations*; Derrida, *Of Grammatology.*
10. Charles Sanders Peirce: "How to Make our Ideas Clear", *Collected Papers,* C. Hartshorne and P. Weiss eds., Cambridge Massachusetts, Harvard University Press, 1931-35, 5.388-5.410.
11. See my *Transition to an Ordinal Metaphysics,* Albany, State University of New York Press, 1980; and *Philosophical Mysteries,* Albany, State University of New York Press, 1981.
12. See Polanyi, *Personal Knowledge.*
13. David Hawkins: "Messing About in Science", quoted in Holt, *How Children Learn,* pp. 128-135.
14. Similarly, "All learning must take place in *potential* space, that is in an unpressurized place and time. Only in such 'space' can a generative system operate and this is what education is trying to bring about". (Robin A. Hodgkin: *Born Curious,* London and New York, Wiley, 1976, p. 59.)
15. John Shotter: "Prolegomena to the Study of Play", *Journal for the Explanation of Human Behaviour,* Vol. 3 No. 1, April 1973, p. 4.
16. Similarly, in a different context: "when anyone faces an area of doubt and reacts to it positively (i.e. not disregarding it or turning away), he enlarges his own field of consciousness and prepares the ground for creative action". (Robin A. Hodgkin: *Reconnaissance on an Educational Frontier,* Oxford, Oxford University Press, 1970, p. 7.)

PART IV

Applications and Conclusion

Introduction to Part IV

The purpose of education is to develop the mind, to expand its powers and enrich its capabilities. At every level, this is attained through query leading to insight, realized in invention and discovery. Learning is the fulfillment of the mind: development of the capacity through discovery to make further discoveries; expansion of the powers of query through further query.

Learning as discovery is a supreme and unconditioned value: that of developing the mind and expanding its capabilities. It competes with other important values, such as justice and personal fulfillment; it is, however, essential to any understanding of these values in human life. Justice and fulfillment depend on understanding for their implementation, but not conversely. In this sense learning is not competitive with, but necessary for, all other important values. It is competitive with other values only in the short run, where we may sacrifice invention to measurable social gain. In the longer run, however, the relations among the supreme values are more complex, since we can understand and encourage other values only where our cognitive powers and understanding have been developed. I will argue that the university's relationship to other important individual and social values depends on its keeping learning and discovery in the forefront of its activities, and that it compromises its other roles as soon as it compromises learning.

CHAPTER 10

Learning and Life

Not only students, but practical people, argue that education is for life; a means to social and economic improvement. University education, they claim, is frequently too abstract, too insular, isolated from the surrounding world. When learning is regarded as a means to an end outside itself, such positions are natural and constitute a dispute over the ends to which social institutions must be subservient. Plato suggests, in his *Republic,* that education is a means to social order and justice. Yet he suggests as well that for the philosopher at least, learning is an end in itself.

The fundamental error lies in the separation of life and learning, as if we might sometimes learn and sometimes live. Learning is the development of the mind. We cannot live without using our minds; conversely, we cannot learn without living. We can, of course, learn many things outside of school; we must also live in many ways while we learn in school. What, then, is the basis for a separation of learning and life? I can find only two plausible interpretations. One is that what is learned in school is thought of minimal value to the lives of those who acquire it. The relevant premise is that learning is always for some extrinsic purpose, rather than the development of cognitive powers and capabilities. Moreover, there is a covert assumption that all learning converges to a common end, as if knowledge were singular not plural, as if there existed one supreme form of query rather than many intersecting but distinct forms. The other

116

interpretation is that the skills and subject matters emphasized in school are not preparatory for success in life but only for success in school itself.[1]

Both views accept the preparatory model of instruction: learning for later application. From this point of view, it is reasonable to question particular applications and goals, suggesting that present social norms are confining and destructive.

Where we reject the preparatory model of learning, and substitute insight and query for memorization and preparation, the plausibility of the criticisms is severely undercut. There are many forms of query, and we may criticize the schools for emphasizing some rather than others. But in every case, query is the process whereby knowledge is acquired and insights are gained. It is the means to and fulfillment of the development of the mind. Extrinsic goals, even of human fulfillment, treat human beings as means to external ends. Learning, as the activity and development of the mind, is a primary exemplification of humanity as an end, fulfilled in its own activities. Query, here, is the realization of the mind, both fulfillment and source of its capabilities. This is the sense in which learning is a supreme value.

It does not follow, as I have indicated, that schools are immune to criticism. To the contrary, they may be criticized for emphasizing certain forms of query at the expense of others. And they may be criticized where they diminish query altogether, and abandon the principle that learning is discovery. I am arguing that the latter failing is the implicit source of most of the standard criticisms: university instruction is far too often preparatory and routine rather than insightful and inventive. I am urging that university instruction should emphasize learning for its own sake as the fulfillment of the mind. This is implicit in the principle that learning is discovery. Before we reject the supreme value of learning, and impose external, practical goals upon instruction, we should consider the possibility that the paradox of learning has warped most instructional activities, and that preparation is commonly substituted for insight, repetition for invention.

The principle that learning is discovery has some important and far-reaching consequences for university instruction. The subordination of instruction to practical ends is far less radical in its implications, for the university has always been subservient to economic considerations and external forces. Emphasis on the mind and its latent powers has fundamental social and political implications. For example, it imposes specific obligations on university participants: to engage in query, to invent and discover. Query has a momentum of its own, grounded in interrogation and invention. Without these, instruction becomes repetitious and confining, discovery is severely limited.

Relevant here is the problem of moral instruction: whether schools have the responsibility of instilling respect for others and a love of virtue in their students. On the basis of the theory of insight, if morality can be taught, it must be grounded in query and suffused with insight. Otherwise it can be acquired only by practice and repetition, habit not understanding—in effect, mindless obedience. How, though, are moral insights arrived at? How are moral discoveries made? These are not questions unique to virtue, but fundamental questions for all education. The universal answer is that learning is discovery arrived at through query and grounded in the powers of the mind.

It follows that for moral instruction as for all other fields of study, learning is gained through query based on insights produced through familiarity gained by experience. The principles of discovery are as vital here as elsewhere: a person makes discoveries where he is familiar with his materials and can work freely with them; he must cross the line between ignorance and understanding many times; he gains insights through his own activities and by witnessing the insights of others. Yet young people are frequently unfamiliar with the features of adult life which moral principles address. They have few major responsibilities; they have made few major commitments. The solution to this difficulty, since unrestricted experimentation with moral principles can be dangerous, lies in the imagination. Through literature and philosophy, history and biography, a person can gain familiarity with events and consequences he has never directly encountered. Direct experience, powerful and valuable as it is, takes too much time and has much too drastic consequences. Literature provides a range of imagination in a variety of experiences not possible in a single person's life—familiarity with remote cultures, times, places, and social classes. It permits experimentation in thought and imagination, if not in life, where consequences are sometimes unremediable.

The exemplary mode of instruction is of great importance here, since we gain insights into the moral values and grounds for action of others only by observing what they do and how they do it. Style is important also, for we understand virtue not only in terms of *what* people do, but *how* they do it, their style of judgment and activity. Imagination can bring familiarity with unexperienced possibilities. Ultimately, however, it is the development of insight, realized through the application of one's own mental powers and the examples set by others, that is the means to moral understanding. Morality and virtue, like all cognitive powers, are gained through query and manifested in the exercise of query—though a mode of query appropriate to them, perhaps unlike other modes.

The question we are examining is whether learning is primarily instrumental to other values—in this case virtue and morality. The answer I am suggesting is that while learning is instrumental, it is a supreme value in itself, and dire consequences follow where we neglect the development of the mind in the interests of other goals. Virtue itself can be acquired and understood only through query, that is, through learning regarded as the natural exercise of the powers of the mind. Moreover, query is useful in an unlimited number of ways: developing the mind, thinking for oneself, achieving precision, taking care, building skills, pursuing ends and so forth. All understanding, including morality and daily activities, requires learning and discovery. In this sense, learning is a necessary and universal means for the pursuit of all other ends. But it is also an end in itself, and a supreme one: the development and enrichment of the mind.

The principle that learning is discovery entails that instruction requires the development of understanding and the encouragement of insight, both realized through unrestricted query. The principle entails reciprocally that research and scholarship—the major forms of discovery—must also be grounded in unrestricted query. The limitations of higher education are, I am suggesting, limitations inherent in the preparatory methods of instruction, and manifest a limited conception of the range of query. Reciprocally, then, query imposes on those who participate in it an unrestricted range of interrogation and methodic response. The limits of instruction are equally limits on research and discovery. As a consequence, an emphasis on learning for its own sake is not a defense of the ivory tower, but a rejection of isolation and withdrawal from the broader range of interrogation query requires. It is entirely a rejection of the preparatory model of instruction; it also entails a criticism of too narrow specializations and arbitrary divisions among branches of knowledge.

Some studies are commonly thought inappropriate to university education. A plausible example is training to become an automobile mechanic. Now the repair of machines is always a form of query. A plausible justification for eliminating such studies from the university cannot be because of their practicality—medicine and law are equally practical—but because of the limited range of such forms of query. Medicine and law encompass a remarkable range of issues and concerns, ethics and justice on the one hand, biology and the mind on the other. The university must emphasize query for its own sake both because such an emphasis can contribute to all fields of human activity, and because it is a supreme value. Such an emphasis entails the neglect of narrow and restricted fields of study. It entails a rejection of overspecialization at both the practical, vocational level and the research and scholarly level. Unwarranted restriction of query is the greatest vice of university activity. The modern university has virtually made a career of that vice, both in instruction and far too frequently in research and scholarship.

The goal of higher education is the development of the mind, and such development is attained through query, which is the exercise of the mind. Nevertheless, there are intrinsic limitations to the university's capacity to develop all forms of insight and understanding, to pursue all forms of query. On the one hand, there are activities which compete with learning for its own sake—political and military campaigns, sports and business. There are forms of query associated with each of these, some of which cannot be pursued in an educational context. Those which can represent one of the most important areas of insight and query, for example, history and political science. But every form of query, including learning for its own sake, has intrinsic limitations. A consequence is a plurality of modes of understanding, irreducible to a common vision. Another consequence is that the university cannot be all things to all men, but is restricted by its own purposes and activities. An emphasis on learning for its own sake is incompatible in certain ways with the pursuit of specific practical ends, even where query is involved. On the other hand, universities are social institutions with modest influence and subject to external forces. Here too limitations are inevitable, in theory and in practice.

As a consequence, universities are beset by conflicting demands expressive of their diverse functions and constraints. They are to provide humanization and equity, insight and training. These are all important values — some far more important than others — but they are in conflict. The supreme values of human life — learning and discovery included — comprise no uniform system of ideal adjustment, but involve continual choices and produce constant tensions. I have suggested that many of the ills of contemporary universities can be interpreted as a concession to the paradox of learning. I am suggesting here that the first and most important step to rectify the ills is to emphasize learning above all, the development of insight and understanding, regardless of where this leads. This will provide that kind of humanization that rests on the cognitive capacities of the mind — in a broad sense inclusive of more than "intellectual" insights. It may include, for example, awareness of all forms of cognitive competence including emotional and social forms of understanding that also depend on insight and discovery. But the university's emphasis on understanding as a primary value will preclude some forms of social practice where extrinsic goals are primary. Equity is inherent in learning and discovery, but so are important inequities in natural capacities. I am arguing that the first and most important concern of the university is learning and discovery, and that where that concern is maximized, many related ills will be ameliorated. Not only is query a supreme value for its own sake, but it has a supreme value for all activities where insight and understanding are involved. Nevertheless, most forms of cognitive activity in daily life are qualified by extrinsic goals. This is the strongest argument for the university's emphasis on query for its own sake, to demonstrate the powers of the mind freed from constraints irrelevant to it, to carry query through in directions emerging from its own imperatives. But as a consequence, the university is limited in its capacity to serve specific social ends: it cannot be all things to all men. It cannot build the mind and also prepare people for specialized vocations, cannot develop understanding and also develop everyday social skills, cannot pursue query and also provide social mobility. The university can build the mind; it cannot provide the solution to society's problems—not if there is no uniform solution.

The somewhat ironic conclusion is that the only avenue toward rational improvement of human life is through untrammeled query, building the mind and providing understanding. For this reason, an institutionalized commitment of the university to query for its own sake, in its many relatively unrestricted forms, is a supreme value instrumentally as well as intrinsically. Yet query itself is pluralistic, involving many different and competing modes; moreover many of the restricted forms of query are incompatible with the pursuit of query for its own sake. The pursuit of knowledge for its own sake has the widest possible consequences for the application of the mind to practical goals of life, but it cannot replace them and it frequently is in conflict with them.

Nevertheless, an emphasis on learning and discovery does eliminate the internal divisions that are destructive to higher education. Only where learning is discovery and understanding is based on insight do we escape from the oppression of external goals to which education is subservient, which foster the regimentation and sterility felt by many students in the classroom. Only an emphasis on discovery and insight can preserve as well as enhance the diversity of points of view essential to query and enriching to educational experiences. Here is the major solution both to the inculcation of virtue and the improvement of social life, not as ends to which query is subservient, but as goals to be realized through the activities appropriate to query. The principle that learning is discovery entails that we come to understand moral principles and how life is to be improved only through query, while query is the union of process and outcome which, divided, makes us sense an opposition of schooling and life.

Part of moral instruction is the inculcation of respect for life and justice. Part of education is adjustment to society and social norms. Part of life is the fulfillment of day to day responses. All of these are very important, but they can be accomplished by habituation and training as well as learning and understanding. We may follow precepts and engage in activities in essentially an unthinking fashion, largely devoid of insight, or we may follow norms and complete tasks with the full attention of our minds, involving insight, invention, and understanding. As Socrates suggests in the *Meno,* only where understanding is involved can we claim to know what we are about in moral affairs, and this requires the full capacity of our minds. The reply to the claim that education is for life is that learning is for itself and thereby is for life, for learning and discovery are among our greatest and most enduring values.

CHAPTER 11

Academic Freedom and Academic Responsibility

Like all social institutions, the university has responsibilities for human welfare and the improvement of the conditions of life. Like all such institutions, it must establish an adequate balance of values which define its larger social importance. Yet the singular character of the university's commitment to learning and discovery gives it a unique social role, and we must examine its contributions to the conditions of life from the standpoint of learning and discovery before we consider its other responsibilities. I have suggested, in fact, that acquiescence in external social values—values other than learning and discovery—diminishes the effectiveness of cognitive powers and ultimately weakens the contributions of the university to social life. From both a human and a social point of view, it is essential that institutional force be given to the pursuit of query for its own sake. On the other hand, such an emphasis is incompatible with an ivory tower mentality. Both the preparatory model of instruction and the ivory tower withdrawal in the name of study for its own sake are restrictive of the powers of the mind, restrictive of questions and of methods of answering them. Query is in principle unrestrictive, and an emphasis on query for its own sake leads both to study at the borders of different branches of knowledge and to criticisms of social policy and events that have produced the forms of knowledge we are habituated to today.

I have suggested that a fundamental element in moral instruction and the inculcation of virtue is the free play of moral alternatives in the imagination. Only by such imaginative invention can virtue become familiar and understood. Even in the case of moral instruction, then, we must learn to accept moral principles for ourselves and discover our allegiances and commitments. Like every other branch of learning, moral instruction is founded on insight and understanding.

We may expand this position in relation to the larger social and political responsibilities of the university. On the one hand, the university may be made subservient to external moral and political standards, for example, stability and fulfillment. Such subordination will always tend to weaken concern for the development of the powers of the mind through invention and query. On the other hand, the free play of ideas in learning and discovery may be made the primary value in university life at the expense, we may assume, of social stability, even well being. We may overcome the sharpness of this opposition by recognizing that the inculcation of social conformity and moral sentiments cannot be preferred where it leads to merely habitual responses, and that cognitive powers of evaluation and analysis are required in all thoughtful moral and social policies.

Learning and discovery are themselves fundamental social and political values. Where moral and political principles are based entirely on traditional and authoritative grounds, they may conflict with the free and open activities of query. A far more plausible position is that morality and politics are themselves forms of query where courses of action are produced through careful investigation and study, where insight and discovery are central factors. Here, then, the university develops the cognitive powers which are exercised in the specific ways essential to action and policy. The limitations imposed on query by moral and political ends can be drastically confining unless they are accompanied by relatively unrestricted forms of query which expand the horizons of the mind and allow us to consider a far wider range of possibilities.[2]

In *On Liberty,* John Stuart Mill argues that in the open and unrestricted play of competitive ideas, what is true will eventually triumph, and it will triumph *only* where there is diversity and conflict of opinion.

...truth has no chance but in proportion as every side of it, every opinion which embodies any fraction of the truth, not only finds advocates, but is so advocated as to be listened to.

Both truth and diversity are supreme values here.

The demand that all other people shall resemble ourselves grows by what it feeds on. If resistance waits till life is reduced *nearly* to one uniform type, all deviations from that type will come to be considered impious, immoral, even monstrous and contrary to nature. Mankind speedily become unable to conceive diversity, when they have been for some time unaccustomed to see it.[3]

Mill's position is a close political analogue of the view of the university I am proposing. Truth and effectiveness in moral and political affairs depend on diversity of thought and invention. Where social life becomes relatively homogeneous and universities are cut from a common cloth, then diversity becomes an evanescent possibility unrealized in the cognitive activities of human beings.

The goal in higher education is learning and discovery for their own sake, teaching so that students may learn, discoveries as the teachers learn. A major implication of this principle is that the freedom which university faculties prize so highly is, as Robert Maynard Hutchins argues, far less a freedom from coercion and far more a freedom inherent in the activities of the mind. The play of ideas upon each other is the court in which all important and enduring discoveries are made.[4] The university has a political and social function of utmost importance merely in being what it is, unconfined by external expectations. What we require is the conviction that free inquiry will lead to truth. This is none other than the premise required in order that we be able to inquire at all; a trust in the powers of the mind on which all inquiry is based.

The implications for academic freedom are profound. We

must conclude that university faculties deserve the greatest possible freedom because they perform a function essential to a free society—that of invention and discovery, the enhancement and expansion of the life of the mind. Yet such a freedom from coercion is largely construed as a species of liberty, though a very important one. Academic freedom is also a freedom inherent *in* the activities of the mind, realized in learning and discovery. This freedom is what makes query possible, and it is manifested in the discoveries which are part of the query.

Human beings who serve the life of the mind can avoid serving existing powers—social and political—only by making learning and discovery primary in whatever they do. The paradox of learning entails the dissolution of the line establishing an unassailable cognitive authority: analogously, the authority of established social and political institutions must be continually challenged. Rich and detailed social criticism is an obligation inherent in the free exercise of rationality. It is a fulfillment of the freedom inherent in the life of the mind. In this sense, then, the university can serve no institutional authorities without compromising itself. It can fulfill its obligations only by untrammeled rational activity, the development of alternatives to all established policies and institutions.

There is only one important freedom: the freedom to know, which is a freedom to think, invent, discover, learn, and most of all, to inquire. Academic freedom is a freedom of the mind and a freedom in thought. The removal of constraints and pressures is only a precondition of a free mind, which must engage itself in order to be free. This conclusion is inherent in the criteria of understanding: insight and invention. A free mind will propose alternatives, make inventions, and arrive at insight.

An important consequence of such freedom is its respect for diversity. We have returned to Mill's value of social plurality. Invention and insight produce plurality and must presuppose its value. Even where query produces universal agreement—as in the sciences—it does so in myriad ways and offers a wealth of modes of expression. Query is committed to plurality and diversity of cognitive activities, and these are inherent in the life of the mind. If academic freedom means anything at all significant within human life, it must involve diversity and plurality of thought and attitude, for these are inherent in the powers of the mind that produce learning and discovery and are a predominant feature of query.

Only one kind of freedom is an unqualified good in university life: the freedom of learning and discovery. Where there is genuine learning and discovery, people are free. And where they are thought free but learn little and make few discoveries, then they are not truly free in their minds.

CHAPTER 12

Conclusion

Education is the development of the mind in a sense involving all the cognitive powers, including bodily capacities and skills, social and linguistic capabilities. The fundamental and general principle of education is that learning is discovery: the development, expansion, and transformation of insight through query. Four related, subsidiary principles are the principles of invention, transcendence, implicitness, and assimilation, all of which are accommodated in the theory of insight. Learning, then, is the achievement and transformation of insight, measured by invention and the ability to go beyond what has been presented, based on a wide range of associated insights which can be expressed only partly at any time and which comprise what a person understands.

Several additional principles are essential to the instructional applications of the theory of insight. These principles involve familiarization, play, and intermittent confusion as we move back and forth over the line between ignorance and knowledge many times. They also include the capacity we have to understand the workings of other people's minds when we observe them in action. These principles define the relationship of teacher and student to learning, which is perhaps the only essential consideration. Insight and understanding are the goal of education; the essential function of the teacher is to encourage the development and enhancement of insight through invention, discovery, and

129

familiarity. As learning is ultimately personal—the acquisition of individual insights—teaching is ultimately a personal relationship. It follows that the most important and effective mode of instruction is the exemplary mode, where the teacher exhibits himself as a primary exemplar of the cognitive powers which he seeks to develop in his students and which he encourages them to develop. Graduate education is clearly exemplary in this primary sense at its most advanced level. Moral and religious education is often exemplary in the same way. So is instruction in performance fields like music, art, and sports. A fundamental reply to the separation of teaching and research is that instruction by example nullifies the separation. The example set by the teacher is dependent on his role as researcher or performer. The importance of invention in understanding thoroughly nullifies the possibility that learning by example might lead to mindless repetition.

The exemplary mode of instruction offers us a resolution of an important difficulty in many contemporary theories of the mind. The reproductive theory of cognitive development tends to make invention and transcendence obscure, and is incompatible with the theory of insight. Yet it does provide a central role for the teacher and for other persons in the development of the mind. Transcendental, neo-Kantian theories which emphasize the innate powers of the mind do not provide a clear role for social relationships in the development of knowledge. Neither Chomsky nor Piaget defines a specific and fundamental role played by parents or teachers in cognitive development. The principle of transcendence here creates an important conceptual difficulty: if the mind advances of itself beyond the available data, including the observed activities of other people, then there is no necessary and central role played by other people in the development of the mind. [5]

The theory of insight resolves this issue by the principle that we have direct and immediate insight into the workings of other minds. Such insight is immediate and direct but no more so than any other form of insight. It is also fallible and often erroneous. The point is that we inevitably transcend what we observe (in a narrow sense) when we observe the cognitive activities of others, and learn from them by example to employ our minds as they do. No theory of cognitive development can be intelligible if it does not rest on a capacity whereby we learn to think by the example of others. We might even describe this mode of insight as a form of imitation except that we are imitating minds at work, not simply repeating what we have observed. The principles of transcendence and invention are fundamental: we observe the minds of others in discovery and we transcend what we observe by gaining insight into different methods the mind can employ. The problem of other minds here is a trivial one: we can function cognitively only insofar as we can understand how other people's minds function, however fallibly and erroneously. The answer to the related question of what it means to possess a mind is also straightforward and trivial: a mind can engage in query, can learn and discover, possesses insight and is inventive. Above all, it offers us an example which we may choose to follow of how to employ our own minds.

The exemplary mode of instruction may be the only truly effective mode wherein insight can be encouraged and displayed. Yet economic and institutional considerations make it difficult to maintain at the scale of contemporary higher education. A plausible conclusion is that university education is defective precisely to the extent that instruction by example is neither expected nor effective. Preparation and memorization replace insight and understanding where the implicit powers of the mind, which can be indicated only by example, are neglected. An emphasis on preparation for later understanding is an explicit rejection of the exemplary mode. I do not believe that class size is of prime importance here, for a mind can be displayed at work in a lecture as thoroughly as in discussion, and there is ample room for student insight and discovery. What is needed, as I have emphasized throughout, is respect for the inventive powers of the student's mind, and while this can be manifested explicitly in a smaller class, it can be made apparent also in larger settings if these are supplemented by other educational experiences.

Nevertheless, institutional and curricular applications of the theory of insight are needed to supplement the pedagogical emphasis on invention and understanding. Three additional principles are relevant to such applications:

1) *Students should have maximal power to direct their learning commensurate with the nature and quality of what they learn.* This is a consequence of the principle of familiarity as well as of a fundamental respect for human cognitive powers. It is in no way incompatible with a required curriculum, for it emphasizes not *what* is to be learned (subject matter), but *how:* methods, insights, and discoveries.

2) *Learning is discovery: insight, understanding, and invention. Facts are but a means to understanding.* The curricular emphasis here falls on the second half. The more important are facts in a given branch of knowledge, the more they must be grounded in insight and understanding.

3) *There is a plurality of truths, ways to truth, insights, and discoveries, and they may not all be coordinated into a total vision of the world.* This principle expresses the openness of query and the development of novel forms of understanding. It is essential to the principle of assimilation, for there must be relevant ways in which understanding varies with person and circumstances, and there is no supreme or objective mode of understanding under which all insights are to be subsumed. This principle of plurality may be the fundamental principle on which all instructional and curricular applications of the theory of insight are to be based.

The principle of plurality has two corollaries. One is that since there is no unified knowledge of the world, but many such kinds and branches, there is no rational ground of unification of all university fields, and every university is more properly a *multi*-versity than a *uni*-versity.[6] Conversely, however, there is no fixed and determinate plurality of branches of knowledge, but many fields with indeterminate boundaries established in part by subject matter but also by tradition, circumstance, and social contingencies. It follows that new insights may be acquired at the boundaries of every field of knowledge. While there is no basis for a general overview of all fields of knowledge as the foundation of a liberal education, there is a continual imperative to investigate new modes of connection and to develop new branches of knowledge through query.

The identification of learning and discovery entails that what is most effective for advanced research must in principle be accommodated at earlier phases of instruction. From the principles enunciated above, a number of examples of curricular and instructional organization may be delineated that will encourage insight and promote understanding. The most important imperative, however, is given by the principle of plurality with its corollaries. There must be a diversity of modes of instruction within and among colleges and universities to provide space for students to familiarize themselves with their work in their own terms and to develop interesting, sometimes important insights. The most effective mode of organization that can accommodate this plurality is where the smallest differentiation is made between teacher and student, expert and novice. We return to the Socratic model again, interpreting it as a collaborative enterprise of learning and discovery, query and further query. Reciprocally, however, the pursuit of knowledge through query entails a wealth of relevant perspectives and an openness to novel possibilities that is incompatible with authoritarian models of both instruction and understanding. There is only query: that is how we advance in knowledge, as experts and as students.

We may return to the fundamental principle that learning is discovery. Invention can be encouraged but it cannot be produced on demand. The greatest discoveries are often least expected. The faith of all education is that learning will occur, that the human mind possesses effective cognitive powers. Discoveries will be made; insights will emerge. All teachers can do is to give of themselves so as to encourage students in their own development. Higher learning is not the formation of young minds, but the inspiration to them to join in the pursuit of truth and excellence in all its forms, even new forms as yet undiscovered.

REFERENCES

1. See Holt, *How Children Fail;* Illich, *Deschooling Society.*
2. I believe this is the primary concern of Heidegger's discussions of our technological age and of his rejection of metaphysics: "We think in too limited a fashion as long as we expect only development of recent philosophies of the previous style. We forget that already in the age of Greek philosophy a decisive characteristic of philosophy appears: the development of sciences within the field which philosophy opened up.
   …is the end of philosophy in the sense of its development to the sciences also already the complete realization of all the possibilities in which thinking of philosophy was posited? Or is there a *first* possibility for thinking apart from the *last* possibility which we characterized (the dissolution of philosophy in the technologized sciences), a possibility from which the thinking of philosophy would have to start out, but which as philosophy it could nevertheless not experience and adopt?"
   (Martin Heidegger: "The End of Philosophy and the Task of Thinking", *On Time and Being,* New York, Harper and Row, 1972, pp. 57, 59).
3. John Stuart Mill: *On Liberty.*
4. Robert Maynard Hutchins: *The University of Utopia,* Chicago, University of Chicago Press, 1953, Chapter IV.
5. See David Hamlyn: *Experience and the Growth of Understanding,* London, Routledge and Kegan Paul, 1978.
6. Though a multiversity in a very different sense from Kerr's in *The Uses of the University.*

Index